The Kids' Guide to

First Aid

All About Bruises, Burns, Stings, Sprains & Other Ouches

Karen Buhler Gale, R.N.

Foreword by David Buchholz, M.D.

Illustrations by Michael Kline

A Williamson **W** *Kids Can!* ® Book

WILLIAMSON PUBLISHING

CHARLOTTE, VERMONT

LIBRARY OF CONGRESS CATALOGING-IN-PUBLICATION DATA

Gale, Karen Buhler, 1961-
   The kids' guide to first aid : all about bruises, burns, stings, sprains & other ouches / Karen Buhler Gale ; illustrations by Michael Kline.
     p. cm. -- (A Williamson kids can! book)
   "Reviewed and approved by a board-certified pediatrician."
   Includes index.
   Summary: A first-aid handbook with instructions on how to handle safely life's "ouches" and how and when to get more help for more serious situations.
   ISBN 1-885593-58-9 (pbk.)
   1. First aid in illness and injury--Juvenile literature. [1. First aid.] I. Kline, Michael P. II. Title. III. Series.

RC86.5 .G35 2002
616.02'52--dc21
                                   2002026772

KIDS CAN!® SERIES EDITOR: Susan Williamson
INTERIOR DESIGN: Sarah Rakitin
BOOK ILLUSTRATIONS: Michael Kline
COVER DESIGN AND COVER ILLUSTRATIONS: Michael Kline
PRINTING: Quebecor World

Williamson Publishing Co.
P.O. Box 185
Charlotte, VT 05445
(800) 234-8791

Printed in Canada

10 9 8 7 6 5 4 3

Little Hands®, *Kids Can!*®, *Tales Alive!*®, and *Kaleidoscope Kids*® are registered trademarks of Williamson Publishing.

Good Times™, *Quick Starts for Kids!*™, and *You Can Do It!*™ are trademarks of Williamson Publishing.

Dedication

To my daughter, Shelby, and my son, Grayson. Without them, it would never have occurred to me to write this book!

Acknowledgments

I would very much like to thank my husband, Peter, who has always been supportive of my dreams; my daughter, Shelby, who was my reader and kid expert; my son, Grayson, who was content to play with his cars while I worked away at the computer; my sisters, Trina Washburn and Mary Buhler, for their enthusiasm; and Kristen Hammond, who provided unfailing child care and is like a member of our family. I am grateful for the understanding and support of my best friend, Gayle Kellner, and many thanks to my dear friend, Forrest Kinney. His early faith in my writing gave me some of my own.

Most important, I must thank my editor, Susan Williamson. She was tireless in her support of the work and has the gift of perseverance with a vision to match. My sincerest gratitude to Jack Williamson and all the people at Williamson Publishing who worked so very hard on the book's behalf. To Dr. David Buchholz — one of the finest (and nicest) pediatricians I know — I extend my deepest thanks for taking the time out of his busy schedule to review the book and write the foreword.

And though it is corny but true, I must thank my little sheltie dog, Tess. Without her quiet, companionable presence at the foot of my chair, the days of writing and researching would have been lonely ones indeed!

Contents

Where's the chapter on tuna?

Foreword

I've been a pediatrician for more than a decade now and, on an almost daily basis, I see kids just like you, often brought in by their parents for a variety of injuries, accidents, bites, and the like. Sometimes the problem is serious and sometimes it's not, but the visits have one thing in common: The family is worried and they're asking for help to make it better.

You've probably taken precautions to prevent being injured, like wearing your helmet, seat belt, and sunscreen. You may have eliminated all the poisons and weapons from your home or, at least, locked them away in a safe place. But despite all of your good intentions and best efforts, "bruises, burns, stings, sprains, and other ouches" sometimes happen, and you'll need some advice on what to do.

The Kids' Guide to First Aid will help you learn some basic first-aid skills that will relieve your worries about what hurts or itches, and it will make you more confident about your ability to make it better. You will learn how to create your own first-aid kit and even a little bit about how the body works. You'll learn some common sense ways to prevent injury and illness, and while you're at it, you might even have some fun.

I'd like to encourage you to take some time to read the whole book (not all at once!), but I would also like to invite you to pay special attention to the prevention information. You should always do what you can to keep yourself and others from getting hurt. But, sometimes, injuries and accidents still happen, so you'll be glad you learned some first aid, too.

I know you'll do your best, but if you don't know what to do, don't be afraid to ask an adult for help. If nobody's around and you think it might be an emergency, call 9-1-1. The 9-1-1 operators are always glad to help, and they'll never be mad that you called.

David Buchholz, M.D.
Chief Medical Officer, PacMed Clinics

4

What a Kid Can (and Can't) Do in an Emergency

Can do

Can't do

First Aid for Kids

is about

➕ **knowing when to get help**

➕ **knowing how to prevent injury**

➕ **knowing how the body works**

so you can take better care of yourself and others.

Does that surprise you? Well, my friend, let's be upfront about this part right from the start: This book is going to teach you a lot, but it won't make you a doctor; it won't make you a nurse; it won't make you an EMT (Emergency Medical Technician). No way! Are we straight about that?

Always GET HELP from a grown-up when you or someone you know is in an emergency situation.

After all, you're a kid — a smart, good kid — but emergencies demand grown-ups, and, usually, professional medical care.

Knowing when and how to GET HELP saves lives.

And that is where *you* come in. There is a lot that you can **observe** and **tell** and **do** that can help make someone more comfortable, prevent an injury from getting worse, and actually save a life:

✚ You can tell a grown-up anytime you or someone else is stung by a bee (page 23);

✚ You'll recognize the signs of infection (page 18) before it becomes serious;

✚ You can perform the Heimlich maneuver when you or someone else is choking (pages 65–67);

✚ You can warn a friend who is at risk for frostbite or frostnip (page 87, 89);

✚ You can tell a grown-up what the snake or spider that bit someone looks like (pages 26, 36, 37);

✚ You can keep a friend calm until a grown-up comes to help;

✚ You can make an AFTER-BITE PASTE (page 24) to relieve itching, an ANTISEPTIC WASH (page 70) to help prevent infection, and a butterfly bandage (page 71) when someone has a deep cut;

✚ You can ask grown-ups to check your home for overheated water that can burn, poisons and medicines that little kids might eat, and improperly stored and prepared food;

✚ You will know when to elevate a wound (blood doesn't like an uphill climb!), when to apply an ice pack (keeps bruising and swelling down in the first 24 hours), and when to apply heat (helps your body clean up the dead cells after an injury).

See? You are already learning what to do when, and we haven't even begun.

So, remember, even though you are not a medical professional or a grown-up, there is a lot you can do, beginning with a call, scream, or shout to **GET HELP** in an emergency. And, please, take care of yourself first. You are that important!

Getting Started With
FIRST AID

F irst aid is great! But can you wait just a bit before you get busy pulling a splinter out of your baby sister or bandaging up your friend's knee? There are some important things to remember so you can be effective and safe, as well as caring and competent!

that the best way to learn about first aid is to take a certified first-aid course through your local chapter of the American Red Cross? A **B**asic **A**id **T**raining, or **BAT,** course is offered for kids ages 8 to 12. It teaches all the basic first-aid techniques, including rescue breathing and the Heimlich maneuver, as well as safety on your bike and on the playground. There are other courses for kids over 12, too, where you can learn advanced life-saving techniques such as CPR (cardiopulmonary resuscitation).

Check in the phone book for the number and address of your local chapter, or visit the American Red Cross web-site at <**www.redcross.org**>. It will help you find the contact information for your local chapter and may also list classes available in your area. What are you waiting for?

Did I mention ... PREVENTION?

Uh-oh, I think this is an emergency!

* **Stay calm.** It's easier to think clearly when you are calm. Plus it reassures the injured person that help, not hysteria, has indeed arrived.

* **Call for help.** Always do this except for the most minor injuries. A grown-up can help you determine how serious (or not) a situation is, or might become.

* **Don't put yourself in danger.** That might make two victims! Call for help instead.

* **Assume the worst.** If you think someone has a broken bone, it is better to assume that they have one and not do further harm.

* **Do no harm.** If you don't know what to do and the situation is not getting worse, call for help and reassure the injured person that help is on the way.

FIRST-AID TRICKS
When It's Serious

If someone is seriously injured, say from a terrible fall, you could worsen his injuries just by moving him. *Unless the person is still in danger (from fire, for example), don't move him.* Keep him calm and lying still. To maintain his normal body temperature to reduce the risk of shock, see page 9. Be comforting and reassuring. That is always a big help!

STAY CALM

Calling 9-1-1

Dial: 9-1-1
Say: This is an emergency!
Explain: Who, What, When, Where, and How Many
Don't hang up!

Preventing Shock

Preventing shock is a very important part of first aid, especially with a more serious injury. Shock is a dangerous failure of blood to reach all areas in your body. It can be fatal. Shock (not electrical shock) can result from many different situations, such as a large blood loss, a severe response to an allergy or bee sting, intense pain, or severe stress. The skin becomes pale, cold, and damp. The person becomes anxious with a rapid heartbeat (detected by checking the pulse, see page 10) and may lose consciousness. Wanna stay shock free? Keep calm and still, cover up or get some shade, depending on the weather, to help maintain a normal body temperature.

EMERGENCY!

The only kind of, sort of, good thing about an emergency is that it usually looks and feels like one! Anytime you think an injury *appears* life threatening or any situation *looks* like an emergency, **ask a grown-up to evaluate the situation, and if necessary, call 9-1-1. If you are alone, shout for help and call 9-1-1!**

Throughout this book you will find sections that say **GET HELP!** These tell you

☞ when to call 9-1-1,

☞ when to go to the emergency room,

☞ when to go to a doctor, and

☞ when to tell a grown-up.

Q & Ask the Nurse

Q: **What is a fever?**

A: I'm sure you know what it feels like to have a fever. Think back to the last time you had the flu. Not only were you achy, but you also felt too warm and maybe had chills.

A *fever* is a body temperature higher than its normal of 98.6°F/37°C. A fever means the body has mobilized its defenses on your behalf against a virus or bacteria. Because of this, a fever shouldn't be treated unless it gets very high. When temperatures go over 101°F/38.3°C, the body is too warm and can't function as efficiently. In this case, cool sponge baths and medicines are used to help bring the fever down. Children tend to have and tolerate higher temperatures than adults do. Another great thing about being a kid!

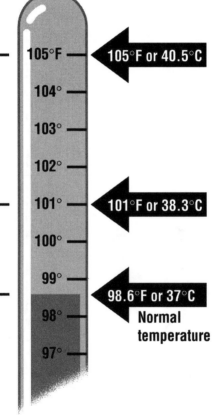

High-grade fevers

Low-grade fevers

105°F
104°
103°
102°
101°
100°
99°
98°
97°

105°F or 40.5°C

101°F or 38.3°C

98.6°F or 37°C
Normal temperature

☑ Check It Out!

The beat goes on

You've got to have a pulse to be alive! There are certain pulse points on your body where you can feel your *pulse* (heartbeat). Taking a **radial pulse** is commonly used to check the heart rate of a person in nonemergency situations. Be sure to use your fingers and not a thumb when checking a pulse point (your thumb has a pulse of its own so instead of detecting someone else's pulse, you'd just be feeling your own. Whoops!)

A weak pulse, a too rapid (over 100 beats per minute) or too slow (below 60 beats per minute), or an irregular pulse often indicates trouble.

To take your own pulse, using your two fingers, apply a small amount of pressure to the opposite inner wrist on the thumb side. Feel it? It should be regular, steady, and strong.

Make-Your-Own Emergency Number Checklist

You'll need: Poster board, markers and pen, adult help.

1. Make a checklist to hang near the main phone in your home. Decorate it with the universal sign of help, which is a large red cross, or with other pictures that will help everyone know that this is important information.

2. Ask a grown-up to help you include accurate information:

For fire, ambulance, or police emergencies: DIAL 9-1-1
(If 9-1-1 is not available where you live, list fire, rescue, and police phone numbers.)

✳ Name of household:

✳ Address:

✳ Your phone number:

✳ Local police:

✳ Poison Control Center:

(Put poison sticker here.)

✳ Parents/guardians/or responsible

adult's work and cell phone numbers:

✳ Family doctor (name and number):

✳ Family dentist (name and number):

✳ List family members with ages and any serious allergies (nuts, bee stings, medicines):

✳ Nearest neighbor (name, phone number, address):

✳ Local hospital medical information line (for nonemergency medical advice after hours):

The red cross, the universal sign of help

Mr. Yuk and the National Capital Poison Center's poison warning symbol

WHAT TO DO

THE HAPPY BIRTHDAY HAND-WASH

Wash your hands *before and after* giving first-aid care. Many germs and diseases — some extremely serious — are transmitted on the skin and especially through bodily fluids like blood. For extra protection, you can buy latex medical gloves (for about 10 cents a pair) to put in your first-aid kit, or you can use plastic baggies as substitutes (but that doesn't mean you don't have to wash your hands anyway!).

Wash before and after handling food, before eating, and after using the bathroom, changing diapers, playing with pets, handling garbage, handling money (it's true!), blowing your nose, sneezing or coughing into your hand, and handling uncooked meat and poultry.

Objective: To wash your hands for 15 seconds so you and your "patient" will stay free of germs and infection.

You'll need: Soap, water (warm is best but any temperature will do), a singing voice.

The water temperature is not as important as being sure you scrub long enough and well enough *with soap.* Sing the first verse of "Happy Birthday," which should take about 15 seconds — just about the right amount of time to get most of the germs. Scrub well in the creases and around the fingernails. Rinse well, too. You want to send the germs down the drain!

Happy birthday to me... happy birthday To me...

Wash BEFORE (unless it's an emergency) and AFTER giving first-aid care.

ℕow you have all the skinny (so you won't be a ninny) when it comes to first aid. Go to it!

MAKE-YOUR-OWN FIRST-AID KIT

First-aid kits contain all the right stuff and with a kit, the right stuff is also in the right place! I mean, who wants to get a jumbo splinter and have to ransack the house to try to find a pair of tweezers?

First-aid kits come in a variety of shapes and sizes, depending on the needs of the person or family using them. You can make the KIDS' GREAT FIRST-AID KIT by gathering up a lot of things that are already in your home (with the permission and help of a grown-up) and putting them in a container. There might be a few things that you'll need to purchase, but they are inexpensive and easy to find at your local drugstore or large supermarket. What can I say? It feels great to be prepared!

Get a grown-up's permission. If you are moving household items to your first-aid kit, you need permission from a grown-up and the owners of the items.

Make the kit available. Tell everyone who is responsible enough in your household (like grown-ups and older siblings) where the kit will be. Then, feel good that even though you might not be able to help someone, your kit can!

Find a suitable container. Here you have lots of choices: Lunch boxes and small plastic toolboxes are nice because they have handles and are water-resistant, but a shoe box or large zip-locking plastic bag could work in a pinch. Improvise, but also consider that it's best if the container is hard-sided, waterproof, and has a handle. Label it in large letters using a permanent marker. You might want to add a red cross, the recognized symbol of first aid.

Find a permanent "home" for your kit. Remember, it should be available to everyone who is permitted to use it, but safe from young children (store it on a higher-up shelf or in a closet). Always return it to the same place.

Check it once a month. Replace what has been used up and be sure supplies like ointments have not expired.

☑ Check It Out! Kids' Great First-Aid Kit

Alcohol wipes (12) or rubbing alcohol and cotton balls: For cleaning needles, clippers, and tweezers.

Aloe vera gel: This is great for any kind of burn or skin discomfort.

Antibiotic ointment: Polysporin or Neosporin are good choices for keeping you germ free!

Band-Aids: Assorted sizes.

Bulb syringe: A small plastic one for flushing cuts or scrapes.

Cotton swabs: For dabbing, cleaning, and applying ointments.

Elastic bandage: A 2"- (5 cm) wide roll to wrap mild sprains and strains.

First-aid tape: To secure bandages, and you can also make your own butterfly bandages (see page 71) with it.

Gauze (pads): Several small *sterile* gauze pads for covering and cleaning cuts and small wounds; 2 or 3 large *nonstick* gauze pads for covering sticky burns and scrapes.

Gauze (roll): A 2" (5 cm) width is good for wrapping an injury on an arm, leg, or finger.

Hydrocortisone cream (1%): When you itch, this is going to help!

*Ice pack: If you can, buy a "break to use" ice pack that turns cold when "broken" or twisted. At home, keep a reusable frozen ice pack in the freezer. Or, substitute a plastic bag filled with ice and wrapped in a cloth anytime; it works just as well as a store-bought pack.

*Note: In this book, when we refer to an ice pack, any of these kinds will work fine. Be sure not to put ice directly on your skin, so wrap your pack in a cloth.

Magnifying glass (small): This is to see your work up close and personal.

Mirror (small): For checking out any eye problems.

Plastic bags (small, resealable): Use these as ice bags in a pinch, or use as plastic gloves if something is kind of icky.

Safety pins: For use with the sling or elastic bandage.

Scissors: For cutting first-aid tape.

Sewing needle: To use with splinters and blisters.

Sling: See pages 113-114 to make your own.

Soap: A small bottle of liquid soap (you can use it even if no water is available).

Soap dish: For storing small items like needle, tweezers, and safety pins. (You could use a plastic bag, too.)

Tissues: Good for bloody noses, tears, and general cleanup.

Tweezers: For all those tweezer-able things like splinters and ticks.

Extras

After Bite Itch Eraser: Buy, or see page 24 to make your own.

Antiseptic wash or a cleanser like witch hazel: Buy, or see page 70 to make your own. Handy if no access to soap and water.

Penlight: To shine a little light on the subject.

Note

We have not included any medicines such as Ipecac (for poisoning), or Benadryl, or even Tylenol. Ask an adult to make sure these are available in *the family's* medicine cabinet, but kids — well, you know the rule: Don't give or take any medications by yourself.

 Mix and match and put together a kit that reflects how you and your family live and play. Being prepared, that's you. Well done!

BEACH BUMMERS

Cuts & Stings from Sea Life

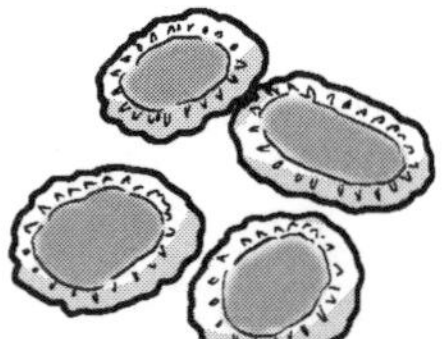

BARNACLES

JELLYFISH

If the beach looks empty except for you, your friends, and your big picnic basket, look again! Lots of marine creatures call the beach and ocean home. If you have ever stepped on a barnacle, sea urchin, or a piece of coral, you know they are reminding you to take good care of their habitat while you are visiting. So don't litter, look but don't touch, and be a good guest!

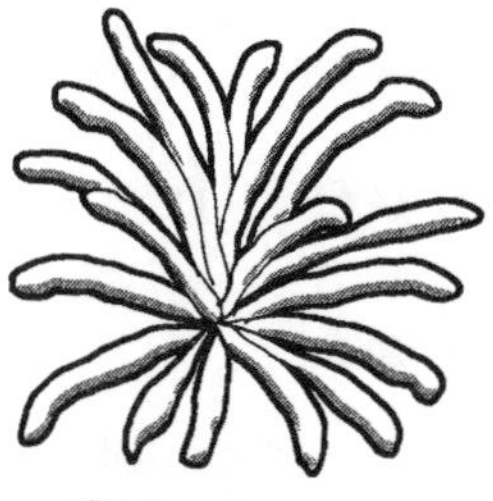

SEA URCHIN

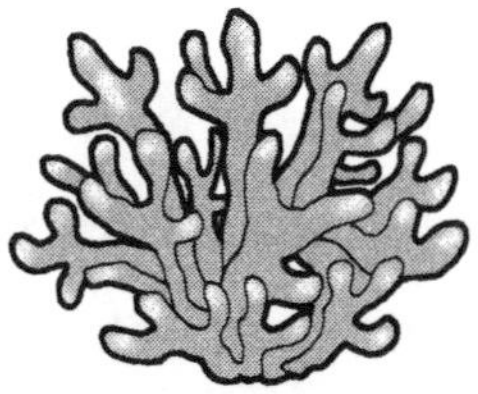

CORAL

DID YOU KNOW..
that these are all living animals, even though coral looks like beautiful and fragile rock, sea urchins like spiny pincushions, and barnacles like bits of white rock?

PORTUGUESE MAN-OF-WAR

Watch out for these critters at the beach!

DID YOU KNOW...

that even if a jellyfish or one of its cousins like the Portuguese man-of-war is lying — *uh!* — dead on the beach, its tentacles can still sting you? It's not fair, but it's true. I would just look, but not touch. How about you?

GET HELP!

TELL a grown-up NOW to TAKE you to the emergency room or to CALL 9-1-1 NOW (if you are alone, CALL 9-1-1 NOW) if you have any of these symptoms after being stung, poked, or stepping on sea life:

☞ muscle cramps
☞ nausea and vomiting
☞ allergic reaction, including shortness of breath
☞ blistering

TELL a grown-up NOW and GO to a doctor TODAY if you have any of these signs of infection over the next few days: increased pain, redness, or swelling; any streaking or milky, stinking drainage (pus); or fever.

Did I mention ... PREVENTION?
A better day at the beach

✱ **Look but don't touch.** Now how easy is that?

✱ **Wear aqua socks or water shoes.** These are any rubber-soled (so the critter's spines can't poke through) flat shoes with a mesh top that you can wear in and out of the water. Amphibious. Great!

✱ **Take a look now and then!** Because of the rinsing and soothing properties of salt water, you may not even know you have cut your foot while you are in the water.

STINGS from Jellyfish & Their Cousins

WHAT TO EXPECT

Pain. A burning and intense sensation. You know, PAIN!

Redness and rash. Like hives — raised itchy spots on the skin. Lumpy bumpy!

WHAT TO DO

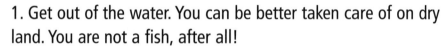

Objective: To remove the stingers from jellyfish and other sea life stings.

You'll need: Salt water, vinegar (or baking soda and water rinse), tweezers or flat object for scraping.

1. Get out of the water. You can be better taken care of on dry land. You are not a fish, after all!

2. Give it a SALTWATER rinse. Not fresh water, as that could make the *harpoons* (little needles with venom sacs attached) squirt even more venom. Don't rub the harpoons with sand!

3. Rinse with vinegar to help prevent the harpoon's sacs from squirting more venom. OK, OK, the vinegar stings a little, but it does the job! Or, you can make a runny liquid of baking soda and water.

4. SCRAPE off the tentacles. Use any flat, thin object (like a library card) or tweezers to scrape (not squeeze, pull, or dig) the harpoons off the skin. Careful not to get them stuck in your hand. Rinse with vinegar again! A grown-up might give you something for the pain. *Don't take or give any medications by yourself.*

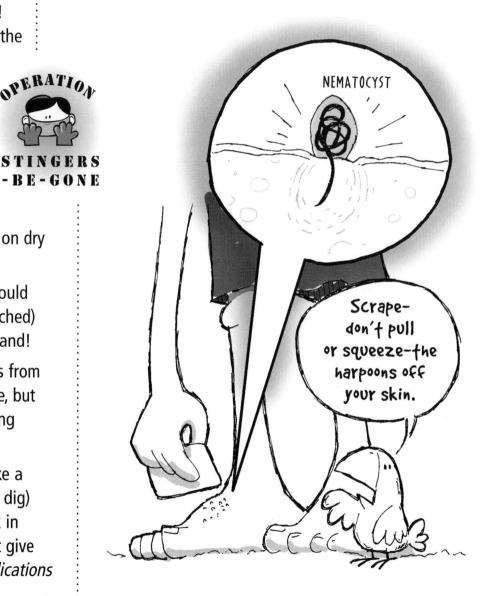

NEMATOCYST

Scrape– don't pull or squeeze–the harpoons off your skin.

CUTS & POKES
Coral, Sea Urchins, Barnacles & Starfish

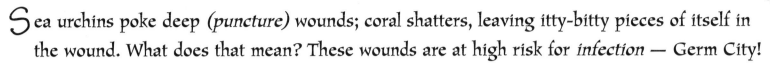

Sea urchins poke deep (*puncture*) wounds; coral shatters, leaving itty-bitty pieces of itself in the wound. What does that mean? These wounds are at high risk for *infection* — Germ City!

GET HELP!

**TELL a grown-up NOW and
GO to a doctor TODAY**

☞ if it's a sea urchin or coral wound.

☞ if you have any of these signs of infection over the next few days: increased pain, redness, or swelling; any streaking or milky, stinking drainage (pus); or fever.

FIRST-AID TRICKS
The Sticky Tape Trick

Got tape? Got itty-bitty coral pieces stuck in your hand or foot? Apply adhesive tape to a coral wound and many of those pieces that are embedded in your skin will lift up and out when you pull off the tape. TA-DA! Applause, please!

There we go. That'll be $387.50.

WHAT TO EXPECT

This depends on how deep the poke or cut and by what creature, but in general:

Pain. Always pain! Not only from the cut, but because some are *toxic.*

Bleeding. Barnacles are like sharp knives — ouch!

Redness and swelling. Always that, too!

WHAT TO DO

Pick out any large pieces or spines. Do this with tweezers so you don't poke your hand!

Stop the bleeding. Apply firm pressure with a clean cloth or gauze. See OPERATION CUT CARE, page 70, for a how-to-do-it illustration.

Rinse with salt water. Called a *marine rinse* to wash out any leftover dirt and debris.

Elevate the wound. It will help reduce the swelling and bleeding.

Tetanus shot? Maybe — maybe not! The bacteria that cause tetanus (see WHAT IS TETANUS?, page 72) live in the ocean, among other places. You may need a shot if it is a nasty wound and your last shot was more than five years ago.

Pain medication. A grown-up might give you something for the pain. *Don't take or give any medications by yourself.*

 SPECIAL HELP for sea urchin and starfish pokes

Soak the wound in hot water for 30 to 90 minutes. **Ask a grown-up to help you.** The water should be warmer than your body temperature (98.6°F/37°C), at about 110° to 115°F (43°–46°C) in order to break down the toxins. Hot, but not hot enough to burn you, because then you'd have two problems!

🐚 Great! You did a good job caring for yourself or a friend. 🐚

BEE STINGS

Poor you and poor bee! Bees don't *want* to sting you; they are only protecting themselves. I mean, you accidentally hit it, stood on it, or (I hope not) *sat* on it. And now you are hurting (poor you), but what about the bee? After a honeybee or bumblebee stings, it dies. Poor bee!

Honeybees and bumblebees leave their stingers behind, so you will need to remove the stinger if it hasn't fallen out on its own.

Wasps and yellow jackets don't leave their stingers behind, so BEE-WARE! They can sting again!

HONEYBEE

BUMBLEBEE

WASP

YELLOW JACKET

22

GET HELP!

TELL a grown-up NOW
to TAKE you to the emergency room
or to CALL 9-1-1 NOW
(if you are alone, CALL 9-1-1 NOW)

☞ if you are *allergic* to bee stings and have been stung.

☞ if you have just been stung by a bee in the throat or mouth and are having trouble breathing from the swelling.

TELL a grown-up NOW if you have been stung by a bee, *even if you have been stung before.* A person can be allergic or *can become allergic* to bee stings at any time — **and this can be life threatening.** This is especially important if you were just stung many times, because there will be more bee *venom,* or poison, in your system.

TELL a grown-up NOW and GO to a doctor TODAY if you have any of these signs of infection over the next few days: increased pain, redness, or swelling; any streaking or milky, stinking drainage (pus); or fever.

WHAT TO EXPECT

Pain. A bee is little, but its poison is mighty!
Redness, swelling, and warmth. Warm, red, puffy skin with a white spot in the middle.
Itching. Baby, oh baby, it itches!

Q & Ask the Nurse

Q: **How do I know if I am having an allergic reaction to a bee sting?**

A: You have probably been stung by a bee before and if you are not already allergic, you probably had the usual symptoms of pain and redness with lots of itching later. All are normal.

In an *adverse,* or allergic, reaction, you might experience tightness in your throat and chest, swelling all over your body including your mouth and lips, a feeling of being dizzy, weak and faint, nausea and vomiting, and hives. And, the swelling around the bite doesn't go away after several days. No fun, for sure!

WHAT TO DO

Objective: To remove a honeybee or bumblebee stinger without injecting any more venom into the skin.

You'll need: Soap and water; magnifying glass; flat, firm object like tweezers or a nail file (part of a nail clipper); ice pack; After Bite Itch Eraser (or MAKE-YOUR-OWN AFTER-BITE PASTE, see below).

1. Wash your hands with soap and water. Using the magnifying glass, look for the stinger — it will look like a small sliver. If the stinger is still in your skin, *scrape*, don't pull, the stinger out.

2. Once the stinger is removed or you are sure it's gone, wash gently around the sting with soap and water. Apply an ice pack or a cold, damp cloth to the area, leaving it there for as long as you can. *Ahhhh! Remember, don't put the ice pack directly on your skin.*

3. Dab on some After Bite Itch Eraser or make your own (see below) to help take away some of the discomfort. But no scratching, please! That just breaks open the skin and "Camp Infection" will set in.

4. Pain medication. A grown-up might give you something for the pain or swelling. *Don't take or give any medications by yourself.*

OPERATION
BEE
FREE

SCRAPE the stinger out gently using tweezers or a nail file.

Make-Your-Own After-Bite Paste

YOU'LL NEED: Spoon, baking soda, cup, water.

1. Mix one spoonful (15 ml) of baking soda with just enough water to make a thick paste.
2. Apply to the stung area and leave on for 15 to 30 minutes. (But wouldn't you have rather made a cake?)

SPECIAL HELP *for people who are allergic to bee stings*

If you know you are allergic to bee stings, you should have an emergency bee-sting kit with you during bee season. The kit will contain either antihistamine pills, or injectable adrenaline, or both to help reduce the symptoms. Have your doctor teach you how to administer the medicine yourself. It could save a life ... yours!

Did I mention ... PREVENTION?

Be sweet, but not a bee treat

* **Be a statue.** Bees don't want to sting. Don't twitch a muscle, and they'll probably fly away.
* **Don't dress like a flower.** Bees love bright colors. Tone it down and they will probably pass you by for your neon-pink neighbor. (Tell her the secret!)
* **No fancy smells.** Yup, this is being a flower again. Sweet smelling includes soaps, perfumes, and even fabric softener! (But you still need a bath!)
* **Use insect repellent that is safe for kids.** Avon's Skin-So-Soft is a good one.
* **Cover up your sweet drink.** Bees love the sweet stuff and will actually crawl *inside* the can or bottle. You need to bee-ware or — *gulp!* — you could get stung on the lips or dangerously in your mouth and throat. Use containers with lids, put something over the top, or pour your drink into a wide-mouthed container. Then, look before you drink. Otherwise, you might have a very buzzy day!
* **Stay away from garbage.** Lots of creatures that sting hang out there. And it stinks, you know!

☑ **Check It Out!**

See it to bee-lieve it!

You'll need:

❀ 3 brightly colored items such as pieces of cloth or paper in bright pink, yellow, orange, etc.

❀ 3 dull colored items in shades of tan, gray, etc.

❀ Perfume, cologne, or aftershave (get permission first; some of this stuff is very expensive!)

❀ Some bees — just go outside in the spring and summer

Color wise! Place the colored objects in a sunny spot about a foot (30 cm) or so from each other. From a few feet (1 m) away (wearing dull colors yourself!), watch to see which colors attract the bees (and butterflies) and which ones don't. You might even get a hummingbird to come calling if there are some bright reds there. Are you glad you dressed in drab?

Mmm! A good smell casts a spell! Spray some of the things with perfume, cologne, or aftershave. Watch from afar how the bees respond even to the drab colors when they smell sweet. Make a chart of the combinations of colors and scents that attract the most bees — and avoid them!

WELL DONE, my good friend. Don't forget to remain calm and be reassuring to someone who has been stung. You are now an official member of the Sting and Rescue Squad!

BITES from Bugs, Spiders & Ticks

Getting bitten is a tiny critter's way of saying that you — your blood, that is — are very tasty, or "Hey! Get your mitts off of me!" (For BITES FROM SNAKES, CATS, DOGS & PEOPLE, see pages 35–41.)

Bugs aren't being mean; they are just living out their natural life cycle doing their three favorite things — eating, growing, and reproducing. Ah, that's the life! Bites are a way of getting food or a way of communicating. So don't get mad — get smart, listen up, and take good care!

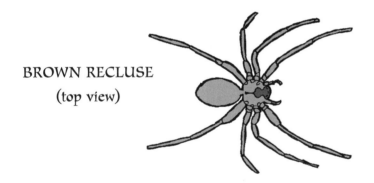

BROWN RECLUSE
(top view)

Have you ever been to my website?

BLACK WIDOW
(female underside view)

The bite is red-white-blue and sometimes develops into a purplish blister. Some people get a fever, chills, weakness, and a body rash.

The bite is rarely painful and causes little swelling or redness. Symptoms of a bite include muscle cramps of the abdomen and back, muscle pain, numb and tingling palms and bottoms of feet, headache, facial swelling, sweating, restlessness, and anxiety.

The Usual Backyard Suspects:
Mosquitoes, Flies, Chiggers & More

WHAT TO EXPECT

A pinprick-sized bite that might hurt a little. Often this is just a tiny spot. Flies, though, tend to leave a painful red bump that may last for a few weeks and chigger bites swell a bit more and turn white after a day or so.

Mild swelling. An alarm from your body that something foreign has entered the skin. Where? Oh, there!

Itching. And lots of it, too. Bet you knew that!

SCORPION

The most dangerous scorpion's bite is immediately and intensely painful, and is made worse by tapping on the site. The less dangerous scorpions have a sting similar to a bee's.

GET HELP!

TELL a grown-up NOW and GO to a doctor NOW

☞ if you have been stung by a scorpion

☞ if you live in the Southwestern United States and you have an unidentified sting that might be that of a scorpion

TELL a grown-up NOW and GO to a doctor TODAY

☞ if you don't know what bit you and you experience more than a mild reaction, such as nausea, vomiting, headache, some swelling of the lips and face, fatigue, or joint pain.

☞ if you have any of these signs of infection over the next few days: increased pain, redness, or swelling; any streaking or milky, stinking drainage (pus); or fever.

DID YOU KNOW...

that with *mosquitoes*, it's the ladies that bite? They need a good fresh blood meal — that's where you and I come in — before they go lay their eggs on still water (like a pond, puddle, or swamp).

Aahhh...

OPERATION BITE-BE-BETTER

···**WHAT TO DO**·················

Objective: To obtain comfort and prevent infection of a bug bite.

You'll need: Soap and water, ice pack, After Bite Itch Eraser or MAKE-YOUR-OWN AFTER-BITE PASTE (see page 24), Band-Aid (optional).

1. Wash your hands and the bite thoroughly with soap and warm water.

2. *Scratch as little as possible.*

3. Ice is nice, so apply an ice pack (or use a cool damp cloth) to the bitten area. *Don't apply ice directly to the skin as it could freeze it.*

4. Apply a dab of an after-bite paste and leave it on for 15 to 30 minutes.

5. Use a Band-Aid to minimize scratching and getting the bite dirty.

Did I mention ... PREVENTION?

Banish those buggers!

✳ **Cover up.** Put some clothes on ... the less skin that shows, the better! Wear light-colored clothes (insects are attracted to bright or dark clothes), thick socks, and sturdy shoes when you go tramping about in the woods and fields. Tuck your pants into your boots or socks.

✳ **Use insect repellent.** Use one that is safe for kids, like Avon's Skin-So-Soft or Buzz Away by Quantum.

✳ **Keep moving.** Even bugs find that it's harder to hit a moving target than one that is standing still.

✳ **Avoid areas with slow-moving water.** They're a bug nursery!

✳ **Stay away from garbage.** You're not a fly!

✳ **Treat for fleas.** Check with a veterinarian about flea-prevention medicines you can give your pet once a month. That's good for you and Fido!

✳ **Don't smell so darn sweet.** Fragrances are in soaps, sunscreen, and dryer sheets — not just perfume — so use them sparingly. Your plain old self smells fine to me!

FIRST-AID TRICKS
Make-Your-Own Bug Repellent

YOU'LL NEED: Water, eucalyptus essential oil (found in natural foods stores, some drugstores and supermarkets), plastic spritzer bottle.

Mix 1 cup (250 ml) of water with 5 drops of the eucalyptus oil. Dab lightly on the exposed areas of skin or put in a spritzer bottle and lightly spray yourself (don't spray your face — dab the repellent on with a cotton ball). Reapply frequently, every 1 to 2 hours, if you get wet or perspire a lot.

Spider Bites

Almost all spider bites are *not dangerous to humans, just uncomfortable and annoying. There are two spiders, however, that are dangerous: the brown recluse and the female black widow (see illustrations, page 26).* They are especially dangerous because their bites are often painless, which means you can get sick and not know right away that these critters did it!

GET HELP!

TELL a grown-up NOW to TAKE you to the emergency room or to CALL 9-1-1 NOW (if you are alone, CALL 9-1-1 NOW) if you think a black widow spider or a brown recluse spider has bitten you.

TELL a grown-up NOW and GO to a doctor TODAY if you have any of these signs of infection over the next few days: increased pain, redness, or swelling; any streaking or milky, stinking drainage (pus); or fever.

WHAT TO EXPECT

A moderately painful bite. Sometimes it's painless, but not very often!
Swelling. Red, puffy, and maybe some mild hardness.
Itching. Notice that everything that bites you seems to make you itch, too?

WHAT TO DO

See OPERATION BITE-BE-BETTER, page 28.

FIRST-AID TRICKS — Make an Immobilization Splint

One way to slow the spread of venom from a poisonous bite is to keep the limb *immobile* (restrained so that it can't move) by fashioning a splint. If the bite is on an arm or leg, you can use (just as you would with a broken bone or a sprain) rolled-up newspapers or magazines, a ruler, or anything else that can be made rigid to immobilize the injured limb. Use anything like the long sleeves of a shirt, backpack straps, rope, a roll of gauze, elastic bandage, belts, or tape to secure the splint.

Q & Ask the Nurse

Q: If a poisonous spider has bitten someone, is there anything she should do on her way to get medical help?

A: That's a great question. Yes, you can help yourself or someone else in the rare case of a poisonous spider bite: The bitten person should be still, apply an ice pack to the bite, keep the bitten area *below* the heart, and if the bite is on an arm or leg, keep it immobile. All these things help reduce the spread of the venom.

Did I mention ... PREVENTION?

Let the spiders be hiders

✳ **Cover up.** See BANISH THOSE BUGGERS!, COVER UP, page 28.

✳ **Apply insect repellent.** See USE INSECT REPELLENT, page 28 and MAKE-YOUR-OWN BUG REPELLENT, page 29.

✳ **Look, but don't touch.** Not touch, then look!

✳ **Shake out clothes and shoes before putting them on.** A spider might be napping in there!

✳ **Stomp your feet.** Spiders such as the brown recluse and the black widow like dark, dry places where there are lots of flies — places like sheds, closets, and the garden. Their favorite place? Outdoor toilets — as if outdoor toilets weren't yucky enough! So stomp around so they'll hide before you, well, go about your business!

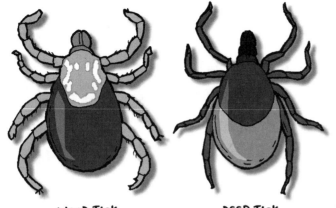

WOOD TICK
(enlarged size)

DEER TICK
(enlarged size)

DEER TICK
The real thing is
smaller than a freckle

Tick Bites

Once ticks get on your skin, they travel to moist and cozy areas like your armpits and *groin* (around your private parts) and your *scalp* (your head and hair), too. Ticks feed by burrowing their heads into your skin and using their fangs to suck blood. It's enough to give you the creeps!

Ticks love the woods and fields. The problem is that they can carry disease from one animal to the next — and that next animal could be you.

WHAT TO EXPECT

Small, generally painless, bite. So far, so good.
Itching. Not so good.
Redness and mild, hard swelling. Called a *nodule,* sometimes this can get quite large and be like a sore. Now, it's a bummer!
Multiple bites or a very large bite can cause fever, chills, and fatigue.

GET HELP!

TELL a grown-up NOW if a tick has bitten you, so she can supervise its removal.

TELL a grown-up NOW and GO to a doctor TODAY

☞ if you develop a rash that looks like a bull's eye — a red dot that grows into a large, roughly circular red area that has appeared anywhere on your body. This could signal Lyme disease from a deer tick.

☞ if you develop a rash of small pink spots on your wrists and ankles that then spread to your body along with a mild fever. You might also have a loss of appetite, headache, and muscle aches, too. This could be Rocky Mountain spotted fever.

☞ if you have any of these signs of infection over the next few days: increased pain, redness, or swelling; any streaking or milky, stinking drainage (pus); or fever.

WHAT TO DO

OPERATION TICK-BE-GONE

Objective: *With a grown-up's supervision,* to remove the tick without causing further damage to the skin or further exposure to tick fluids. That little bugger has got to go!

Read this carefully before you try to remove a tick. You don't want to leave its head or any other parts of the tick behind, since it can still hurt your skin or make you sick.

You'll need: Soap and warm water, tweezers, alcohol wipe, magnifying glass, antibiotic ointment.

1. Wash your hands with soap and warm water. Clean the tweezers with an alcohol wipe and don't touch the cleaned end after that.

2. Using the magnifying glass, get a good look at the tick in good light. Using the tweezers, grasp the tick *close to its mouthparts and pull it* straight out *with a slow and steady motion. Do not twist, crush, or squeeze the tick.*

3. After the tick is removed, look carefully on the skin for any remaining head parts and *scrape* them away gently with the tweezers, not your fingers. (You don't want to come in contact with any tick fluids.)

4. Get rid of the tick by flushing it down the toilet — *whoosh!* Clean the skin thoroughly with soap and warm water and apply a small amount of antibiotic ointment.

PULL STRAIGHT UPWARD.

Do not twist, crush, or squeeze the tick.

While the tick is on the skin, **don't try to smother it, burn it, or kill it.** This will only cause the tick to throw up more infectious fluid into the wound.

THROW UP?!

Did I mention ...
PREVENTION?

Tick tricks

✳ **Cover up.** See BANISH THOSE BUGGERS!, COVER UP, page 28. Light-colored clothes both protect you and make it easier to spot ticks on your clothes.

✳ **Apply insect repellent.** See BANISH THOSE BUGGERS!, USE INSECT REPELLENT, page 28 and MAKE-YOUR-OWN BUG REPELLENT, page 29.

✳ **Do a tick search.** After you come in from an area where there are lots of ticks, like the woods, do a tick search. Check yourself carefully from head to toe and don't forget the groin area (the skin around your private area). Ask someone to check your hairline (edges) where ticks would most likely latch on.

✳ **Take a shower.** It's kind of hard to miss a tick in your birthday suit!

 Well, there's no doubt about it: You are the Bug Master. Go forth and heal!

BITES
from Snakes, Cats, Dogs & People

Snakes usually have one thing to say to us humans — DON'T TOUCH ME — and unfortunately only one way to say it — CHOMP! Dogs, cats, and kids have one thing to say, too: BE NICE! So, be nice, and you should manage to stay big-bite free!

Snakebites

Most snakes are just slithery, legless guys and gals out and about in the great outdoors. So, don't panic, because most snakes are harmless and want to slip-slide away to be left alone. And, I say, just let 'em! If they could talk, what would they say? You got it — GO AWAY!

BUT THERE ARE TWO TYPES OF SNAKES THAT ARE POISONOUS, WHICH MEANS IF THEY BITE YOU, YOU CAN GET REALLY SICK OR DIE. They are CORAL SNAKES and PIT VIPERS — which include WATER MOCCASINS (also called the COTTONMOUTH), RATTLESNAKES, and COPPERHEADS. Pit vipers are the most common source of bites in the United States and Canada.

GET HELP!

TELL a grown-up NOW to TAKE you to the emergency room or to CALL 9-1-1 NOW (if you are alone, CALL 9-1-1 NOW) if a poisonous snake or an unidentified snake has bitten you or someone else. **If you do not know what kind of snake it is, assume that it is poisonous and call 9-1-1. Don't try to take care of the snakebite yourself.**

LOOK CAREFULLY at the SNAKE if you can. Don't touch a dead snake because the fangs of a poisonous snake can still be dangerous. Be ready to describe what the snake looked like, so it can be identified. This is very important so the doctor will know what type of antivenin medicine and how much to give.

WATER MOCCASIN

COPPERHEAD

RATTLESNAKE

CORAL SNAKE

The Kids' Guide to First Aid

Q & Ask the Nurse

Q: If a poisonous snake has bitten someone, is there anything he should do on his way to get medical help?

A: Yes. Be still and keep the bite *below* the level of the heart. *Don't apply ice to the wound or attempt to suck out the venom (like you see in the old movies).* With a poisonous snakebite, ice can damage the skin and sucking out the venom doesn't really work. So don't pucker up!

Otherwise, follow the instructions for making an IMMOBILIZATION SPLINT (page 30) to inhibit the spread of venom.

GET HELP!

TELL a grown-up NOW and CALL a doctor TODAY if the snake has been positively identified by a grown-up as *nonvenomous*. Treat the wound (see page 38). These bites often become infected.

WHAT TO EXPECT

Poisonous snakebites

Fang marks. The fangs of a poisonous snake often leave a particular pattern.

Pain. Often a burning pain.

Changes in sensation. Numbness, twitching, tingling, sweating, etc. of the affected limb within 30 to 90 minutes, along with problems throughout the body.

Nonpoisonous snakebites

Fang marks. The pattern is different from that of a poisonous snake (although it is difficult for an amateur to tell the difference).

Pain. Of course!

Swelling. Typically there is some swelling.

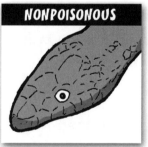

Triangular head and slitted eyes (except coral snakes)

Tapered head and round eyes

FANG
—puncture
/ wounds

WHAT TO DO

Remove yourself from risk immediately. **If it is absolutely, positively, without a doubt, no-way a poisonous snake,** do this first aid and then consider seeing a doctor to further prevent infection. If the bite involves your hand, foot, or a joint, see a doctor. *All snakebites need adult help.*

✓ **Wash, wash, wash.** Use soap and warm water to wash the wound. You know the drill!

✓ **Apply an antibiotic ointment.** A little dab will do ya.

✓ **Apply a Band-Aid.** Use a nonstick bandage and first-aid tape if a Band-Aid is too small.

✓ **Tetanus shot? Maybe, maybe not!** Check with your doctor. If it has been more than five years since you had one, you will most likely need another one to protect you from tetanus (see WHAT IS TETANUS?, page 72).

Did I mention ... PREVENTION?
Put the brakes on snakebites

✸ **Don't touch a pet snake** unless you have been taught how to handle one, you know it is harmless, *and you have the permission and supervision of a grown-up.*

✸ **Don't touch any snake in the wild.** Enjoy nature by simply observing it: It's kinder to the wild creature and better for you!

✸ **Keep your hands out of holes.** Stumps and hollow logs are wonderful snoozing places for snakes.

✸ **Use a walking stick.** Rustling things in front of you and on the other side of logs sends a snake on its way.

✸ **Wear boots and long pants in snake country.** Hard to bite through all of that!

✸ **Wear gloves when going to the woodpile.** Snakes love it there!

✸ **Stand still when you see a snake.** If you don't move, the snake is most likely to slither quietly away. Bye-bye.

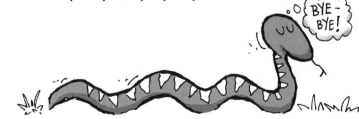

Dog, Cat & Human Bites

Most large bites are from dogs. Not that most dogs are biters, but a cat is more likely to scratch, and a kid is more likely to yell at you!

People are often bitten on the hand by a strange dog that they reach out to touch. Bites are often the last effort animals have at communicating that they would very much like you to keep your distance. That's easy enough, so ... just do it!

Grrrr...*

* stay away!

WHAT TO EXPECT

Pain. How much depends on how bad the bite is and whether or not — ouch! — it broke the skin.

Swelling. Whether or not the skin is broken, the pressure will cause some redness and puffiness.

Bleeding, if the bite broke the skin. Bleeding will be greater if it is more than just a puncture wound from one of the teeth. It also might require stitches if the wound is large or gaping.

WHAT TO DO

See Get Help! on page 39 for any dog, cat, or human bite. Then, if it is minor, care for the wound and consider seeing your doctor.

See Get Help! on page 39

Objective: To reduce discomfort and help prevent infection in a small and minor bite. Then, consider seeing your doctor.

You'll need: Gauze or clean cloth to stop the bleeding, soap and water, antibiotic ointment, Band-Aid or gauze pad and first-aid tape, ice pack.

1. Being bitten is frightening, partly because it is so unexpected. Remain calm so you can think more clearly about what needs to be done. Take some deep breaths — in and out. Good.

2. If there is bleeding, stop it by applying pressure to the site with the gauze or cloth. You may need to experiment to find the most effective pressure spot. Press firmly, using the palm of your hand, and raise the injury *above* the level of the heart, if possible, since it is hard to bleed uphill! Do this for 2 to 5 minutes, or until the bleeding stops.

3. Once the bleeding stops, or if there is no bleeding, wash the wound thoroughly with soap and warm water, but be careful not to dislodge the *clot* (the clump of blood cells that acts like a plug in the bleeding blood vessel) that has stopped the bleeding. Then, soak the wound in warm, soapy water for 15 to 20 minutes.

4. Apply a small amount of antibiotic ointment and a bandage if the bite broke the skin. If a Band-Aid is too small, use a gauze pad and secure it with first-aid tape.

5. Apply an ice pack either to the bandage, or, if the bite did not break the skin, directly onto the skin. Keep the wound elevated with the ice pack on to help reduce the swelling.

6. Tetanus shot? Maybe, maybe not. Talk with your doctor. If it has been more than five years since you had one, you will most likely need another to protect you from tetanus (see What Is Tetanus, page 72).

(see What Is Tetanus, page 72)

Apply pressure to the wound and raise the injury above the heart.

The Kids' Guide to First Aid

FIRST-AID TRICKS

Positive Pressure

Anytime you apply pressure to the site of a bleeding wound, you help to prevent the outflow, or loss, of blood by creating a dam. With the dam in place, the blood can more quickly make its sticky web of cells that will heal over the blood vessels and eventually stop the bleeding.

WHEN BLOOD ESCAPES, IT ACTUALLY CAN BE HELPFUL (IN MODERATION, OF COURSE!). It bathes the wound with both helper cells that clot the blood and white blood cells that eat up germs. Gobble, gobble!

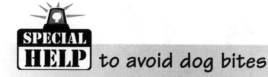

SPECIAL HELP to avoid dog bites

Dogs really are man's and woman's best friends, but sometimes they do act aggressively. Here's what to do at those times:

Be still when a dog comes up to you. A dog tends to chase, so don't run like prey, but be a statue. More than likely, it just wants to give you a good and thorough sniff.

Avoid looking directly into the dog's eyes, which it might think of as threatening. Beware of the dog, but don't *glare* at the dog.

Use a firm voice with a stern command (act as if you are the boss) to snap a dog out of a headlong rush. Say "Sit" or "No!" or "Go home!" If the dog obeys, *back up* slowly and very far away.

Get flat, if you think a dog is really coming at you to do you harm or if you are afraid of dogs and can't be the boss. Lie down on the ground and cover your ears and head. Again, the odds are you are just going to get the Big Sniff!

Now you are really ready to get bit — but please don't. Take good care of yourself and others. You certainly know how to do it!

BLISTERS

Bubble Trouble

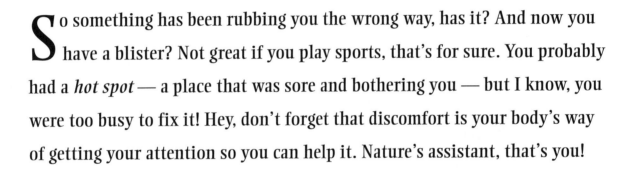

So something has been rubbing you the wrong way, has it? And now you have a blister? Not great if you play sports, that's for sure. You probably had a *hot spot* — a place that was sore and bothering you — but I know, you were too busy to fix it! Hey, don't forget that discomfort is your body's way of getting your attention so you can help it. Nature's assistant, that's you!

HEY!
We need some
HELP down
here...

Hi.
We're blisters!

And I'm a sister blister...

Q & Ask the Nurse

Q: What is a blister?

A: A *blister* is a fluid-filled sac with just the thin, top layer of skin covering it. It develops from too much *friction* (rubbing back and forth) against your skin. The little blood vessels called *capillaries* get weak and leak a fluid that is part of blood.

Your feet tend to get blisters because, although your feet are unique, your shoes aren't — and there's the rub, so to speak! But your hands can get blisters, too — in fact, anywhere something rubs your skin for a long time is susceptible to blisters.

Make a hot spot (almost)

Rub your hands together vigorously for a few seconds. Do you feel the heat? Friction, created by rubbing your hands together, resulted in that heat. If a few seconds of hand rubbing can create all that heat, think what your shoe can do to the side of your poor little toe or heel!

✚ GET HELP!

TELL a grown-up NOW and GO to a doctor TODAY if you have any of these signs of infection over the next few days: increased pain, redness, or swelling; any streaking or milky, stinking drainage (pus); or fever.

A blister (of course!). Skin isn't meant for all that rub-rub-rubbing, and your blister means, "Stop that now!"

Discomfort. You know how blisters can hurt if you have ever been hiking and gotten a blister, but had to keep moving along … *yee-ouch!*

Redness. This should disappear in a day or two as the blister heals.

FIRST-AID TRICKS

Duct Tape

You know, that gray, sticky tape in the garage that's strong enough to swing on. If you apply it *beforehand* to the areas that are prone to getting blistered, the duct tape will create a No-Blister Zone. Be sure to take it off as soon as you no longer need it *while the tape is warm and easily removed.*

Did I mention … PREVENTION?
So you want to be blister free …

Let's face it! Blisters are a drag. But the great thing is, they are rarely anything serious except for the elderly or for people who have an illness that requires special foot care. The other good news is that you can almost always prevent blisters from happening in the first place. So, take care of your feet now, because they gotta go wherever you go!

✷ **The right shoes.** Be sure they are not too loose or too tight, or they are going to rub, my friend. If you can afford it, be sure to get the proper shoes for your sport and break them in a little bit at a time. No hiking up Mount Everest or playing World Cup soccer the first day you get them!

✷ **The right socks.** Wear acrylic (not cotton) socks with heels, or wear a double pair, if they don't make the shoes too tight.

✷ **Powder up.** Use baby powder or talcum powder. Drier feet are less likely to blister (less friction), and hey, they smell a whole lot better, too!

✷ **Fix the hot spot.** Do this pronto — before the damage is done! (See FIRST-AID TRICKS, this page, and MAKE A MINI-DONUT BANDAGE, page 45.)

TO POP OR NOT TO POP?

Let's take a look.

Not pop: If the blister is smaller than a quarter, protect it with a Band-Aid or a MINI-DONUT BANDAGE to prevent further rubbing. The blister is self-contained and won't get contaminated with bacteria. After a few days, the fluid will get sucked back up through the blood vessels and the skin will heal over. It's your body taking care of you! Cool!

Pop: If the blister is as large as a quarter or larger, see OPERATION POP (page 46).

Already popped: If the blister beat you to the pop, wash your hands and follow step 3 of OPERATION POP (page 46).

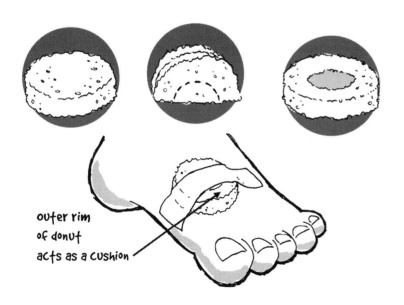

outer rim
of donut
acts as a cushion

FIRST-AID TRICKS

Make a Mini-Donut Bandage

OBJECTIVE: To make a clean, protective circle that will absorb the rubbing, instead of your blister. The bandage shouldn't touch the blister itself. Use for any pre-blister hot spots, too.

YOU'LL NEED: Scissors, small piece of soft fabric foam (like in pillows) or large cotton ball, first-aid tape.

1. Cut out a circle of foam that is a bit larger than the blister. Then, fold the circle in half, and cut out a section from the middle to make the donut hole. (No foam? Use a *large* cotton ball instead.)

2. Place the donut so the hole is over the blister and secure with a piece of first-aid tape. Be careful the tape doesn't stick to the roof, or top, of the blister. (You can use a piece of gauze or loosely pulled apart cotton ball to protect the roof before applying the tape.) The outer rim of the donut will act as a cushion and take the rubbing, not your skin. Good work!

Operation POP

If the blister is as large as a quarter or bigger, it's better to pop it under very clean conditions now than to wait for it to burst in your dirty sock next week! It doesn't hurt, because the skin is dead (may it rest in peace), so there are no nerves to send any pain complaints to your brain. Don't you wish that were true when you stub your toe?

Objective: To pop the blister under clean conditions to avoid possible infection from an open wound.

You'll need: Soap and warm water, alcohol wipe (or rubbing alcohol and cotton ball), sewing needle, sterile gauze or clean tissue, antibiotic ointment, large Band-Aid or small sterile gauze pad and first-aid tape.

1. Wash your hands thoroughly with soap and warm water. Gently wash the blister area, too. Clean the needle by wiping it with alcohol. Don't touch the sharp end once it is cleaned.

2. Gently squish the fluid in the blister to one side, using the gauze or tissue. Holding the needle at an angle, make a tiny pinprick away from most of the fluid. LOOK OUT! Just kidding, it's not really going to splash on you! Leave the flap of skin (roof) over the blister to help protect against germs.

3. Apply a pea-sized amount of antibiotic ointment and then a Band-Aid. Make sure the edges cover the blister, so the adhesive won't pull on the roof. Band-Aid not large enough? Use a gauze pad and secure it around the edges with first-aid tape like a picture frame.

Congratulations! You are almost ready for medical school!

You're the Blister Boss now. Teach what you know to others and take good care of yourself or a friend!

BLOODY NOSE

So much blood! That's the first thing you think of when you get a nosebleed. It's everywhere and it's warm, sticky, bright red — and, well — scary. Blood is supposed to stay *inside* your body, not rush outside to worry you, splashing your clothes so you look like a character from Fright Night!

Alternative Medicine for Nosebleeds — the Chinese Way!

Acupressure is a Chinese system of healing where pressure is applied to specific energy currents on your body to relieve symptoms elsewhere in the body. To see if it works for you, press firmly on the spot between your nose and upper lip for 30 to 60 seconds. Does the bleeding slow or stop?

See no blood   Hear no blood   Bleed no blood

Your friends   your nose

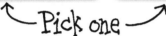

Pick one

GET HELP!

**TELL a grown-up NOW
to TAKE you to the emergency room
or to CALL 9-1-1 NOW
(if you are alone, CALL 9-1-1 NOW)** if the nose-bleed is a result of a severe injury to the head.

TELL a grown-up NOW and GO to a doctor NOW if the bleeding hasn't stopped after 15 to 20 minutes of treatment (including nose spray).

TELL a grown-up TODAY if you are having frequent nosebleeds, prolonged nosebleeds, or you are bleeding from other places (like your gums).

Did I mention ... PREVENTION?
Know what the nose knows

✳ **Quit picking your nose!** Bet you've heard that one before! Not only is it bad manners, but you also can scratch the inside of your nose or pull away a clot (OPERATION BITE CARE, page 40) and then what happens? A bloody nose!

✳ **Blow gently.** Your nose isn't a trumpet. Take it easy!

✳ **Stock up on vitamin C.** This vitamin helps build strong blood vessels. Eat lots of foods high in vitamin C such as citrus fruits (oranges and grape-fruits), pineapple, tomatoes, berries, dark green leafy vegetables (spinach, etc.), and peppers. C'mon, you must like one of those!

✳ **Keep it moist in there.** A nose that gets too dry cracks inside and then what have you got? A bleeder! Using a humidifier or saline nose drops (see MAKE-YOUR-OWN SALINE NASAL SPRAY, page 50) may help in dry, hot climates or in the winter when the heat is on indoors.

✳ **Play it safe!** Rough housing can result in getting bonked on your honker — and sometimes, a little bonk will do ya!

WHAT TO EXPECT

Blood coming out your — nose! The medical term is *epistaxis.* The blood might trickle down the back of your throat and taste salty and … well … bad. (How does Dracula stand it?)

WHAT TO DO

Don't panic. You *aren't* going to bleed to death. You won't even be minus a pint!

Objective: To stop the flow of blood from your (or someone else's) nose quickly and safely.

You'll need: Your fingers, cold washcloth (optional), tissues, soap and warm water.

1. As soon as your nose begins to bleed, pinch it shut with your fingers at the soft, lower part of your nose. Lean forward so the blood doesn't trickle down your throat into your stomach (making you sick). Do this for as long as you can, or about 10 minutes. The longer, the better. Find something quiet to do to pass the "pinching time."

2. Some people place a cold washcloth on the back of the neck to help *constrict* (narrow) the blood vessels, slowing the bleeding.

3. With a tissue in hand, slowly quit pinching and see if the bleeding has stopped. If it hasn't, give it a bit longer. If it has stopped, continue sitting quietly so that the newly formed clot stays in place!

4. Wash your hands thoroughly with soap and warm water any time you come in contact with blood, either your own or others', since certain diseases are transmitted by contact with blood.

OPERATION
**SLOW-
THE-FLOW**

Pinch nose for about 10 minutes to stop the bleeding.

Check It Out!   ## Blood works

Your body is making new blood constantly so that you have the same amount in your system at all times.

Objective: To figure out how much blood you have in your body, based on your body weight.

You'll need: To know your body weight, an empty gallon (3.7 L) milk or water jug, water, measuring cup, pencil and paper.

Every 15 pounds (7 kg) you weigh = 1 pint (500 ml) of blood.
For example, if you weigh 60 pounds (27 kg), here's how you figure it:

60 pounds = 4 pints blood (60 ÷ 15 = 4) = 2 quarts = ½ gallon
27 kg = 2,000 ml blood (27 ÷ 7 = 3.85 x 500 ml = 1,925 ml) = 1.9 L

Now, figure out how much blood you have, based on your weight (get math help if you need it). Fill the jug with the same amount of water. See, there's a lot, isn't there? And you thought you didn't have a *drop* to spare!

Now nosebleeds won't scare you because you've got the inside information—so to speak. Nicely done!

 **FIRST -AID TRICKS** ## Make-Your-Own Saline Nasal Spray

YOU'LL NEED:
¼ teaspoon (1 ml) table salt
1 cup (250 ml) warm water

1. Mix the salt and water together. Make a new batch every three days.

2. Ask a grown-up for an empty nasal spray bottle (thoroughly washed out and rinsed in hot water). Fill it with the homemade SALINE NASAL SPRAY solution. Squeeze three to four sprays into each nostril as often as needed. Ahh! Nice and moist now.

HELPFUL HINT: To warm up the drops, just run the bottle under warm (not hot) water for a few minutes before spritzing into your nose.

BURNS
Hot Topics!

If it's hot, it can hurt! Sun and fire (dry heat) and steam or hot liquids (moist heat) can burn your skin — and your eyes, hair, and lungs, too. But that's not all. There are chemical burns and electrical burns, and even lightning and *radiation* (a kind of energy wave) burns that can zap you, leaving you red and crying. Most burns are minor, thank goodness, and can be prevented. But accidents *do* happen, so here's *what* to do if they do!

DID YOU KNOW...

that doctors can repair severely burnt, damaged, or even missing skin — Hey! Where'd it go? — with a process called *skin grafting*? Healthy skin is cut from the chest, thigh, abdomen, or lower part of the neck or behind the ear, and then *grafted* (sewn) onto the damaged area. It's best if the graft is from the person's own body, which prevents the body from rejecting the tissue as an intruder. You weren't using that skin behind your ear anyway, were you?

I do **NOT** want to play with **YOU.**

Burns from Fire & Other Stuff

GET HELP!

TELL a grown-up NOW to TAKE you to the emergency room or to CALL 9-1-1 NOW (if you are alone, CALL 9-1-1 NOW)

☞ if you have any kind of burn over a large area of your body.

☞ if you have lots of blistering or skin damage.

☞ if you have burns or blisters in your mouth, on your face, hands, or genitals (private parts).

☞ if you have burns that have turned the skin white and hard.

☞ if you have inhaled extreme heat or smoke. Your throat and lungs may have been burned.

TELL a grown-up NOW if you have received a minor burn.

TELL a grown-up NOW and GO to a doctor TODAY if you have any of these signs of infection over the next few days: increased pain, redness, or swelling; any streaking or milky, stinking drainage (pus); or fever.

☞ For burns from fire or hot liquids, **see pages 53–55.**

☞ For a sunburn, **see pages 56–58.**

☞ For burns from chemicals like strong cleaners, **see pages 59–61.**

SPECIAL HELP for burns

The juice from the leaves of the common aloe vera plant is known to reduce pain, prevent infection, and heal burns. Confirm with a grown-up that the plant is an aloe vera. Break off a leaf — be careful of the thorns — and split it open. Apply the juice to the burned area. If you don't have a plant, use the aloe vera gel commonly found in drugstores and supermarkets.

aLoe Vera

WHAT TO EXPECT

The result of a burn depends on *what has burned you* and *where you have been burned.* If you took a big gulp of too-hot soup, your tongue will hurt, sting, and feel rough to the touch. A scald on your arm from a spilled pot of boiling water will leave you with a burn that requires emergency medical care.

Pain. There are millions of nerve endings in your mouth and on your skin, so the message is going to come through loud and clear: Hey! You're cookin' us here!

Skin damage. Depending on how serious the burn is, this can vary from redness to blisters to peeled skin.

FIRST-AID TRICKS

Slurp, then Splash

If you have a minor burn that hasn't broken the skin, you want to cool the skin down right away to limit the extent of the burn. Cold water is best, but sometimes it isn't right nearby. Good news! Any cold liquid will do — iced tea, soda, lemonade, etc. Splash it on; then, rinse with cold water when you can.

WHAT TO DO

OPERATION NO-ICE COOLDOWN

This is for minor burns — those burns that have caused pain, redness, and maybe a small blister or two.

Objective: To cool down the skin and limit the extent of the burn *without using ice.* Ice is not used in treating burns because it can cause further tissue damage.

You'll need: Cold water, all-purpose moisturizing lotion (no creams), aloe vera gel (optional, but recommended).

1. Get away from the source of the burn; then immediately run cold water over the burned area or place it underwater. Do this for 10 to 15 minutes. If there are blisters, see BLISTERS, pages 42–46. Small blisters should be left alone since they are your own best defense against bacterial invasion.

Don't put butter, grease, oil, or any cream or ointment on a burn. It holds the heat inside your skin — the opposite of what you want!

2. *After the burn has been cooled,* and if there are no blisters or broken skin, use moisturizing lotion to soothe the area and help replace some of the moisture. Aloe vera gel is an excellent choice (see SPECIAL HELP FOR BURNS, page 53).

3. A grown-up might give you something for the pain. *Don't take or give any medications by yourself.*

Run cold water over burn or place it underwater. Do not apply ice.

☑ Check It Out!

The hot water inspector

When is hot water a health hazard? When it's too hot and coming out of a faucet! So, turn down the heat!

Ask a grown-up to locate the thermo-stat on your hot water tank. Tell her it should not be set any higher than 120°F (49°C). Turning it down will save energy (and money), too!

Did I mention ... PREVENTION?

Beat the heat!

Most burns happen at home in the kitchen or the bathroom — often to younger kids or elderly people.

✳ **Don't play with fire — EVER!** This includes matches, lighters, and campfires. Most everything can burn — including you!

✳ **Turn on the cold water first.** Then, add the hot water to get it to a comfortable temperature.

✳ **Test the waters.** Use your finger to make sure the water isn't too hot before you take the plunge — in the bathtub, shower, or sink!

✳ **Don't use the stove, oven, or microwave unless you have been taught how to do it safely and have a grown-up's permission.** Hey, that rule applies to just about everything!

✳ **Check hot foods.** Let them cool and take a small taste first. Microwaved foods are especially tricky since the food is heated unevenly. No big mouthful of food — there could be a really hot spot!

✳ **Keep hot liquids away from table and counter edges.** No accidental spills on your pet iguana or baby sister!

✳ **Keep pot and pan handles away from the edge of the stove.** This can prevent a very common and extremely dangerous accident.

✳ **Sip and sit.** Sip hot drinks while sitting still. No live, wiggly creatures on your lap when sipping, either!

Sunburn

The sun's rays are hottest between 10 A.M. and 4 P.M. Those are good hours to wear sunscreen with an SPF (Sun Protection Factor) of at least 15 and to stay covered up. It's very important! Plus, you can't be naked ALL day!

Did I mention ... PREVENTION?

Make sunlight be less bright!

* **Wear sunscreen.** Duh! Not only can using sunscreen prevent you from discomfort now, it can also prevent you from getting skin cancer later on. Winter sun can burn, too, and sun that is reflecting off water, snow, sand, or concrete can burn you even more quickly. Cloudy days can still be burn days, too. Slather the sunscreen on — your skin is counting on you!

* **Cover up.** Do this especially during the peak burn hours. If your freckles are showing up, it means you are getting too much sun. And cover your ears, a common site for skin cancer. Don't forget sunglasses — jeepers creepers, they're your only pair of peepers!

WHAT TO DO

Objective: To cool down the skin to limit the extent and discomfort of the sunburn.

You'll need: A shower or bathtub; calamine, aloe vera gel, or an all-purpose moisturizing lotion; "bath boosters" (optional): ¹/₂ cup (125 ml) cornstarch or baking soda, or one packet of Aveeno colloidal oatmeal.

1. When you get a burn, the first thing to do is cool it (and keep it that way!). If you are away from home, soak a T-shirt in cool water and wrap up in it. At home, take a cool shower or bath. Add one of the "bath boosters" above to draw out more heat.

2. As soon as the skin is cool, rub in some calamine, aloe vera, or moisturizing lotion. Reapply this frequently. If you have blisters or blisters that have popped, see TO POP OR NOT TO POP?, page 45. Remember to leave small blisters alone.

3. Drink lots of liquids because sunburns are *dehydrating* (draws water from the body).

4. A grown-up may give you something for the pain. *Don't take or give any medications by yourself.*

Take a break from the sun for at least a week. Until it heals completely, your skin will be super sensitive and can easily burn again. *Sizzzzzzzle!*

OPERATION NOT-SO-HOT

GET HELP!

TELL a grown-up NOW and GO to a doctor TODAY

☞ if you have lots of blistering over a large area of your body.

☞ if you have a severe burn on your face, hands, or genitals (private parts). There are medications to help reduce the skin's reaction to the burn.

SPECIAL HELP with sunscreens

Use a sunscreen with a SPF of at least 15, and apply it (lips and ears, too) 30 minutes before you go out (including under T-shirts). Reapply it after swimming or excessive sweating, or after two hours, because it washes or wears off. Use fragrance-free, hypoallergenic (not likely to cause allergic reactions in people) sunscreens.

 ## Check It Out!

Make a sunscreen tattoo

You'll need: Cotton swab, sunscreen, your skin, sunny day.

Use a cotton swab dabbed in sunscreen to make a design or to write your name on the back of your hand. Go about your fun in the sun with your hand exposed to the sun (and out of water) for a safe amount of time. (Wear sunscreen as usual on the rest of your body.) Watch the tattoo — which has not been exposed to the sun because of the sunscreen — appear. Great stuff, that sunscreen is!

Chemical Burns

Common household cleaning products that contain bleach or ammonia can be dangerous on the skin and in the eyes. Garden chemicals are also dangerous.

GET HELP!

EYES — SHOUT for HELP and then **immediately rinse out the eye(s) thoroughly** *before* **telling a grown-up to TAKE you to the emergency room or to CALL 9-1-1 NOW (if you are alone,** *rinse eyes first;* **then CALL 9-1-1 NOW)** if you have been splashed in the eye(s) with a chemical.

See OPERATION EMERGENCY EYE-WASH, page 60. *It is extremely important to care for your eyes first! All chemical splashes to the eye are considered an emergency.*

SKIN — SHOUT for HELP and then remove **the chemical from the skin NOW.** It is very important to get the chemical off the skin ***first!*** **See OPERATION SCRAPE-AND-WASH, page 60.** Then, **TELL a grown-up NOW and GO to a doctor NOW.**

This depends (as with all burns) on what chemical burned you and where the burn is. But, in general:

Burning. Very intense, too.

Pain. Skin and eyes are very sensitive and they let you know!

Tissue injury. This can range from mild irritation to a more severe injury that burns through the skin or seriously damages the eye.

EYES:

Objective: To rinse an eye *immediately* and *thoroughly* in order to reduce or prevent damage from exposure to a chemical.

1. **Do not rub your eyes.**

2. **If one eye is affected:** Tilt head to the side of the injured eye and flush with warm (not hot) water from the nose side outward. Do this thoroughly and for 15 minutes. **If both eyes are affected:** It is easiest to rinse them in the shower where you can flood them both.

3. After rinsing, cover the eye(s) with a soft cotton bandage or clean cloth and seek emergency medical help.

SKIN:

Objective: To clean the skin *immediately* and *thoroughly* in order to reduce or prevent damage to the skin from exposure to a chemical.

1. **If the chemical was a powder**, scrape it off first and then rinse the area. **With any chemical exposure,** immediately *wash it off* using cool water. Do this thoroughly for 15 to 30 minutes. *Be careful the water stream is not so forceful that it could spray into your eyes.*

2. Make sure you have removed any contaminated objects touching your skin, such as clothes or a watch or other jewelry (and wash them thoroughly before wearing again).

3. If the skin starts to burn after stopping the rinsing, start rinsing it again. Wrap the area lightly in a clean cloth or bandage and see a doctor now.

Did I mention ...
PREVENTION?

Be clean without a scream!

✳ **Yes, you can still do the dishes!** But never use any chemically based products without instruction and permission first.

✳ **Steer clear of harsh chemicals completely.** If special harsh garden or chemical cleaning agents are being used, stay away! They can splash and cause serious injury.

✳ **Ventilate!** If harsh chemicals are being used or you are using chemically based art supplies indoors, open the windows or work outdoors instead.

✳ **Post the Poison Control Center's phone number near your phone.** Poison Centers deal only with the medical problems associated with poisons and chemicals. Call and tell them what chemical or poison is involved, and they will tell you what to do.

> But MOM—the dish soap has chemicals in it!

 Well done, my friend. You can beat the heat with the best of them!

CHOKING
Remember to *Chew!*

There is a universal sign (everyone knows it) to use if you are choking and cannot get enough air. It is hands on the throat with fingers and thumbs stretched out. It means EMERGENCY! I NEED HELP! And here's where your first-aid know-how can make a big difference — and even save a life.

This sign means

CHOKING EMERGENCY! I NEED HELP!

GET HELP!

*The *Heimlich maneuver* is a way to create pressure in the body so foreign objects that are stuck in the throat can be pushed out.

When someone else is choking:
SHOUT for HELP and then DO the HEIMLICH MANEUVER* even if the universal choking sign is not used *if someone who is choking cannot cough or talk, feels faint, or turns very pale, white, or blue from lack of air.* **See page 65.**

SEND SOMEONE TO CALL 9-1-1 or have someone give care while you call. People can lose consciousness if they don't get enough air within a short amount of time.

When you are choking:
IF YOU are ALONE and YOU are CHOKING, YOU can do the HEIMLICH MANEUVER on YOURSELF. See page 66.

When a baby under 1 year old is choking:
SHOUT FOR HELP, SEND SOMEONE TO CALL 9-1-1, and DO the HEIMLICH MANEUVER on BABIES under 1 year old *if a baby is choking and cannot breathe, talk, cry, or cough; faints, or turns very pale or blue from lack of air.* **See page 67.**

Chew, Baby, Chew!

When something "goes down the wrong pipe," or you choke, it means that instead of going into your *esophagus* (eh-SOF-a-gus), food or other matter has gotten into your windpipe, called your *trachea* (TRAKE-ee-a). Usually, it's nothing that good old coughing and gagging doesn't bring, *uh*, back up! But if the piece is large enough, it could get stuck. What then? You might not be able to get enough air into your lungs because there is a big, old honking piece of hot dog stuck in there instead! So chew, baby, chew!

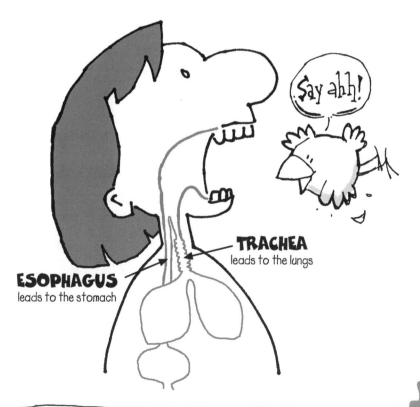

A feeling of something stuck in your throat. Gag!
A feeling of panic. After all, you can't breathe very well!
Forceful coughing. *This is a good sign.* It means you are getting enough air and can most likely *expel* (get rid of) the stuck piece on your own.

I'm not sure if he's choking, or he just tasted a dog biscuit.

SPECIAL HELP **for performing the Heimlich maneuver**

Smart and willing as you are, it is still best if this technique (and most others) is learned as part of a certified first-aid course. The American Red Cross offers a **B**asic **A**id **T**raining (**BAT**) course for kids. Call your local American Red Cross chapter to see if it's available in your area or check it out on the World Wide Web at <**www@redcross.org/services/ youth/teens/opps.html**>.

Did I mention ... PREVENTION?

Don't choke! It's no joke!

* **CHEW!** That's what those pearly whites are for! And really chew your meat — the number one thing people choke on.

* **Clam up.** When you have food in your mouth, that is. No talking!

* **Keep the wee ones safe.** Kids under 3 years old put just about anything in their mouths — food or not! Keep the kiddies away from anything that could become a "plug," such as:
  * any tiny toys or toys with small parts that could break off, aluminum foil, uninflated balloons or part of popped balloons
  * large pieces of food such as: grapes; wads of raisins; raw carrots and celery; large spoonfuls of peanut butter; hard candy; thick, sticky candy like caramels; nuts; large chunks of meat or hot dogs. And all of that goes for you, too, you know!

* **Don't put weird or large stuff in your mouth for a joke.** You know, marbles, 18 grapes for chipmunk cheeks — you get the idea!

Keep coughing! If the person choking can talk, breathe, or cough forcefully, then just let him keep doing it! It's the body's natural and *best* defense coming to the rescue. Let it work!

Do the Heimlich maneuver only in an emergency if someone who is choking

☞ **cannot talk, breathe, or cough,**
☞ **has turned very pale, white, or blue from lack of air, or**
☞ **has given the universal choking sign.**

Objective: To expel a foreign object that is stuck in the windpipe or throat with the use of thrusts.

1. **Stay calm.** Stand behind the choking person and put your arms around him. Have the person bend slightly forward from the waist.

2. With one hand, make a fist and place it just above his belly button. Grab your fist with your other hand. **Press hard, quickly,** and **upward** toward the chest — these are the *thrusts*.

BEND AT WAIST

WITH FIST AND HAND ABOVE BELLY BUTTON, PRESS HARD, QUICKLY, AND UPWARD

3. **Repeat the thrusts** until the object is expelled or emergency medical help arrives.

If you are alone and choking, and cannot cough, talk, or breathe, or you feel faint:

OPERATION
SELF-HEIMLICH MANEUVER

☞ Try to stay calm. Put your fist above your belly button and grab it with your other hand. Do the thrusts on yourself as shown.

OR

☞ Lean over the back of a chair (or a railing, etc.) to imitate the thrusts, placing the chair's edge at the same point above your belly button. Now, do the thrusts using the chair as your hands.

THE SELF-HEIMLICH MANEUVER

☑ **Check It Out!**

Heimlich demonstration

You'll need: Drinking straw, wad of paper.

The Heimlich maneuver uses the pressure in the lungs to push the object out.

Imagine the straw is your windpipe. Plug the straw with the paper. If you try to breathe naturally through the straw, the paper (the choking object) blocks the windpipe. The Heimlich maneuver creates high and sudden pressure, much like blowing very forcefully on the straw. Zoom — the paper wad shoots out! The windpipe (straw) is now clear!

PAPER   BROCCOLI

The Kids' Guide to First Aid

Heimlich Maneuver for Babies under 1 Year Old

1. Turn the baby over on your lap. With the baby's head lower than her bottom and holding her securely with one hand, **give 5 quick slaps to her back.**

2. If the object does not pop out, turn the baby over and place your fingers just below her breastbone and her nipples, and **give 5 quick pushes.**

HEAD LOWER THAN BOTTOM/ 5 QUICK SLAPS

PLACE FINGERS JUST BELOW BREASTBONE AND NIPPLES/ 5 QUICK PUSHES

3. Then, look in her mouth and, **if you can see an object,** try to *sweep** it out with your finger. **Be careful that you do not push the object farther into her throat.**

***Note:** To sweep, gently scoop around the inside of the mouth from one side to the other, using one of your fingers.

4. **If you can't see the object and the baby is still not able to breathe,** start again with the back slaps (step 1) and the chest compressions (step 2) until the object is expelled or emergency medical help arrives.

SWEEP THE OBJECT FROM THE THROAT

Excellent job on learning first aid that could save a life — including yours!

CuTS, ScRAPES, SCRATCHeS & BrUiSeS

Ouch! That hurts!

Your skin is the largest *organ* in your body. It not only protects your body from bacteria and harmful rays from the sun, it also keeps you from drying out like a prune; maintains your body temperature so you don't cook; alerts you to sensations like hot, cold, or gooey; and *excretes* (gets rid of) salt and water so you are not a human sponge! And that's not all! It also makes vitamin D from sunshine and without that, your bones would be soft and warped!

GET HELP!

TELL a grown-up NOW to TAKE you to the emergency room or to CALL 9-1-1 NOW (if you are alone, call 9-1-1 now) if you have a very large cut with a lot of bleeding that does not stop with elevation and pressure. It is possible that you might have cut a larger blood vessel.

TELL a grown-up NOW and GO to a doctor NOW if the wound is fairly large and dirty, or the edges are far apart. You might need stitches and/or a tetanus shot (see page 72) if your last shot was more than five years ago.

TELL a grown-up NOW and GO to a doctor TODAY if you have any of these signs of infection over the next few days: increased pain, redness, or swelling; any streaking or milky, stinking drainage (pus); or fever.

WHAT TO EXPECT

A slice through the skin. Something sharp has made its mark.
Bleeding. How much depends on how big and how deep.
Pain. Your body's alarm (couldn't it call instead?).

Did I mention ... PREVENTION?

Help skin win!

* **Be careful out there!** Never leave your house or do anything fun ... just kidding! But do follow safety rules and look before you leap!

* **Cover up.** Clothes put a layer between you and the sidewalk!

* **Get trained.** In using a knife, in doing a sport, in whatever new skill you are learning.

* **Use recommended safety equipment.** Bike helmets are not optional! Nor are knee and elbow pads, gloves — you name it, wear it!

WHAT TO DO

OPERATION CUT CARE

Objective: To treat a small cut or scratch so it can heal without complications.

You'll need: Gauze or clean cloth, soap and water, antiseptic wash, antibiotic ointment, Band-Aid.

1. Stop the bleeding first. Using a gauze square or a cloth, apply strong pressure to the bleeding site. Also, elevate the wound (because it is much harder to bleed uphill, against the force of gravity). You may need to do this for a minute or two to help the blood clot (see OPERATION BITE CARE, page 40).

2. After the bleeding has stopped, wash your hands and then gently wash the injured area with soap and water. (You don't want it to start bleeding again.) Rinse with antiseptic wash and let dry. Apply a small dab of antibiotic ointment and cover with a Band-Aid. Well done! Change the Band-Aid daily and keep the cut clean until it heals in three to five days.

APPLY PRESSURE TO THE CUT AND ELEVATE THE WOUND TO STOP THE BLEEDING.

FIRST-AID TRICKS

Make-Your-Own Antiseptic Wash

Soap and water work great for cleaning wounds, but for added protection, or if clean water isn't available, use an antiseptic wash. You can make your own using these oils, which are available from natural foods stores, pharmacies, and some large supermarkets.

YOU'LL NEED: Water, a clean jug (quart/liter) with a lid, 4 to 5 drops essential tea tree oil, 4 to 5 drops essential geranium oil.

Pour the water into the jug and mix in the oils. Tighten the lid and store out of direct sunlight. Shake well before using to rinse and wash wounds.

SIMPLE CUT:
NO BUTTERFLY
BANDAGE NECESSARY

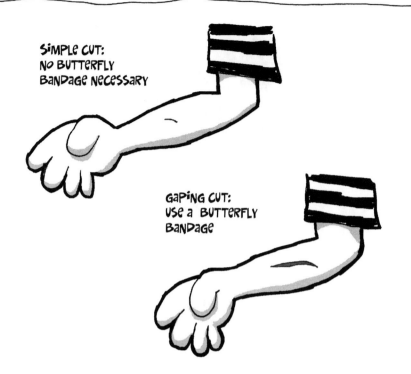

GAPING CUT:
USE a BUTTERFLY
BANDAGE

Make-Your-Own
Butterfly Bandage

If you get a gash or a cut that is a little deeper, with edges that are not next to one another, you may need to apply butterfly bandages. These help pull the skin together and reduce the chance of scarring and infection.

YOU'LL NEED: First-aid tape, scissors.

First, take care of the cut (see OPERATION CUT CARE, page 70). To make a butterfly bandage, fold over a 3" to 4" (7.5 to 10 cm) piece of first-aid tape (without letting it stick together). Snip off a triangle of tape from both folded corners. Place the X (butterfly) part over the cut, pulling the skin edges together.

Snip off triangle of
tape from both corners.

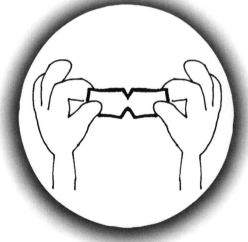

Open to reveal X.

Place the X over the cleaned
cut, pulling edges together.

Q & Ask the Nurse

Q: What is tetanus?

A: It's an illness caused by bacteria found in dirt and many other places. The bacteria can find their way into cuts, particularly deep puncture wounds, and cause a stiffening and paralyzing of muscles. You've probably been told to be careful about stepping on a nail or cutting yourself on sharp metal because you could get tetanus. One of the early symptoms of tetanus is a stiffening of the jaw muscles, so it's sometimes called *lockjaw*.

SPECIAL HELP with shots

If you don't like shots, you aren't alone. Even doctors and nurses who give shots all the time can be wimpy when it comes to getting one! (I know what I'm talking about …) But a large cut that has gotten very dirty or an injury from a dirty nail may require a tetanus shot.

Tetanus, my friend, is much worse than getting a shot, so if the doctor says you need one, then get it. Skip the screaming and squirming, and ask for some ice. Rub it on the skin in a circular motion until the skin is numb. (It's OK to put it directly on your skin for a minute or two if you rub it.) Then the poke will seem more like a joke … ha ha!

Scrapes

GET HELP!

TELL a grown-up NOW and GO to a doctor TODAY

☞ if the scrape is very large or too painful to be cleaned thoroughly.

☞ if you have any of these signs of infection over the next few days: increased pain, redness, or swelling; any streaking or milky, stinking drainage (pus); or fever.

WHAT TO EXPECT

A rash-like wound. There'll be some bleeding and oozing.
Pain. More than you might think. Lots of nerve endings were exposed as you slid on down the driveway! What are they saying? *OWWWW-CH!*

LOOK OUT!

Cuts, Scrapes, Scratches & Bruises

WHAT TO DO

Objective: To clean a scrape so that it can heal without complications.

You'll need: Gauze or a clean cloth for cleaning, soap and water, tweezers, alcohol wipe (or rubbing alcohol and cotton balls), magnifying glass (optional), hand towel, antiseptic wash (see page 70), small cup, clean bulb syringe, antibiotic ointment, gauze and first-aid tape for bandaging (optional).

1. Stop the bleeding by applying pressure with a clean cloth or gauze and elevating the wound, if you can. Wash your hands with soap and warm water. Rinse the wound with soap and warm water, or soak the wound to help remove the dirt.

2. Clean the ends of the tweezers with an alcohol wipe and don't touch the ends after that. In good light, examine the scrape with the magnifying glass. Use the tweezers to pluck out the large pieces of dirt and debris. Ah, souvenirs!

3. Use a small, clean piece of gauze to brush across the wound, scraping away any smaller remaining bits of dirt. Be gentle. This might make it bleed again.

4. Place a towel under the injury. Pour some antiseptic wash into the cup. (If you don't have antiseptic wash, use water.) Suck up the wash into the syringe, and squirt the wound with the wash (it's under pressure, which will help dislodge any remaining debris). Repeat several times.

5. Pat it dry with clean gauze. Apply a small amount of antibiotic ointment. *Leave the scrape uncovered unless it will be exposed to lots of dirt.* It's OK to apply a light bandage of gauze secured with first-aid tape, if you take it off at bedtime.

6. A grown-up might give you something for the discomfort. *Don't take or give any medicines by yourself.*

bRuIsEs

WHAT TO EXPECT

A thump to the body that breaks blood vessels under the skin. Sometimes you don't realize you have been hurt until a few days later when you have a black-and-blue spot!

Skin discoloration. Your skin won't just be pink. It will be blue and purple; then, green and yellow, as the blood cells die and are eventually carried away. Bye-bye!

Discomfort. An ache or tenderness when you touch it ... so don't touch it!

WHAT TO DO
A BRUISE IS A BRUISE IS A ...

Treatment for a bruise, whether it's on a shinbone or an eye, is the same (except you can blow your nose if the bruise is on your leg!). So to treat a bruise, see THE GOOD-BYE BLACK-EYE CURE, page 83.

GET HELP!

TELL a grown-up NOW and CALL a doctor NOW if someone suffers a blow to the eyes or head, or a hard blow to the abdomen. There may be serious injuries to the brain and internal organs without any outward evidence.

TELL a grown-up TODAY if you get lots of bruises without being aware of hurting yourself. This could be a sign of an illness.

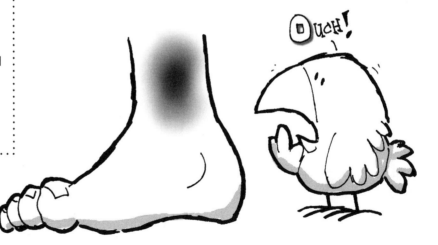

 NEXT TIME YOU OR SOMEONE YOU KNOW GETS HURT, STEP ON UP AND HELP THEM OUT. YOU'LL KNOW JUST WHAT TO DO!

that sound waves pass through your ear canal to your eardrum, which is attached to three tiny bones called the *hammer, anvil,* and *stirrup?* Those bones vibrate and send along those vibrations as nerve impulses to your brain. Your brain interprets that as sound. So here's the scoop: the louder the noise, the rougher the vibration. If it's too rough, it damages all the miniature mechanisms in the ear that let you hear.

So keep it down!

EARS & NOSE
WHAT'D YOU SAY IS IN THERE?

S o you fear
there's something in your nose or ear?
Well, let's peer (and not sneer) —
maybe a bug or bead or something queer
has found its way in theer!

HAMMER ANVIL EARDRUM STIRRUP COCHLEA

I hate opera!

GET HELP!

TELL a grown-up NOW and GO to a doctor NOW if an object is stuck in your ear or nose and cannot be easily and safely removed. The doctor has tools to remove it painlessly.

TELL a grown-up NOW and GO to a doctor TODAY

☞ if your ear is really hurting or it drains fluid or any blood. There are lots of reasons why your ear can hurt, such as an ear infection, buildup of wax, or *swimmer's ear* (irritation from constant exposure to moisture).

☞ if you have any of these signs of infection over the next few days: increased pain, redness, or swelling; any streaking or milky, stinking drainage (pus); or fever.

Psst! I want to put a bug in your ear...

No!

WHAT TO EXPECT

Pain or an uncomfortable sensation that something is stuck in there. Sometimes little kids won't even remember getting stuff stuck in their ears or nose, but you big kids should, *uh*, know better. Bugs, beads, pebbles, beans, peas, paper, cotton — all kinds of stuff can get in there!

Loss of hearing. If there is something plugging the ear canal, the sound waves can't get through. "What'd you say?"

Discomfort, drainage, or fever from a forgotten foreign nose object. Kids, I tell ya!

WHAT TO DO

Foreign Object Removal from Ear

Objective: To safely remove a foreign object from the ear. *If the object is a bug, see page 79.*

You'll need: Soap and water, tweezers, alcohol wipe (or rubbing alcohol and cotton balls), mirror, heating pad (optional and with grown-up supervision only).

1. Wash your hands with soap and water. *Don't poke around in your ear with a cotton swab or tweezers if you can't see the object.* You might just push the object deeper into the ear and possibly injure your eardrum.

2. Instead, turn the affected ear to the floor and use gravity and some shaking of your head to see if the object can be loosened and perhaps fall out. Don't slap your head, though — that will just hurt. Duh!

3. No luck? Clean the ends of the tweezers with the alcohol wipe and then don't touch the ends once they're cleaned. Now, look in the mirror. If you *can* see the object and it is a soft and tweezer-able thing — and you are sure you can pluck it out — go ahead and pluck! Ah, that's better. If you have some discomfort, you can use a warm heating pad (with permission) over your ear for comfort. *Oooh-ahhh!*

Did I mention ... PREVENTION?

Just DON'T do it!

* **Don't stick stuff in your nose or ears!** That's easy *not* to do!
* **Don't let other people stick stuff in their nose or ears — or yours!** Watch for little kids who like to put things in their mouth, ears, and nose.

Hey! Is that an Aggie?

GROWN-UP HELP REQUIRED!

Objective: To safely float a bug out of the ear.

You'll need: Olive, mineral, or baby oil for pouring into the ear, small pan, clean bulb syringe or spoon, tissues.

Warning: Don't use oil in your ear if there is drainage or blood coming out or for anything other than a bug.

1. When there is a bug in the ear, people often feel movement or hear a buzzing sound and feel a tingling sensation. That's strange, but stay calm.

2. Ask a grown-up to warm up the oil in the pan to a comfortable temperature. Test it on your fingertip and then your lip **to be sure it is only warm** (about body temperature) — not hot — and won't harm your ear. Squeeze the bulb of the syringe to fill with the oil.

3. Tilt the problem ear up toward the ceiling. Pull the earlobe up and back to help straighten out the ear canal. Ask a grown-up to put a small amount of oil into the ear while you hold the lobe. The bug should suffocate from lack of air and float out. Whew — what a relief!

OPERATION
EAR
DEBUG

☑ Check It Out!

In stereo

We hear in stereo. That means it takes both of our ears to detect sound and to determine where it is coming from. Throughout your day, alternate covering one of your ears. Is it difficult to hear where a sound is coming from? Are you missing quieter sounds that others are responding to? Ears, like eyes, work as a team. It's a good thing they both get along!

I hate mineral oil...

WHAT TO DO

Objective: To safely remove a foreign object from the nose. There are important things *not to do* as well as *to do* when something is stuck in your beak, so to speak.

You'll need: Tissues, mirror, tweezers, alcohol wipe (or rubbing alcohol and cotton balls).

1. **Don't** breathe in forcefully to try to get the object into your throat where it can be swallowed. It could end up in your lungs instead.

2. **Don't** poke around if you can't see the object. You'll just jam it farther in and that could hurt your delicate little sniffer!

3. *What should you do?* Blow your nose moderately hard to see if you can zing the thing out. If it doesn't shoot out, look in the mirror and see if you can see the object. If you can, clean the ends of the tweezers with the alcohol wipe and then don't touch the ends once they're cleaned. If the object is something soft and tweezer-able — and you are sure you can grab it easily without pushing it farther into your nose — use the tweezers to pull it out.

4. Stop if the object seems to be going deeper into your nose and try blowing again. The, *uh,* mystery object, should make its appearance on cue. TA-DA!

How did THAT get in there?

CONGRATULATIONS! YOUR EAR HAS NOTHING TO FEAR, AND NOW YOU KNOW WHAT THE NOSE KNOWS. SO, KEEP THEM ALL CLEAN AND CLEAR!

Jeepers! Creepers! Take Care of Your Peepers! EYES!

Eyes. They are the windows to your soul and your windows on the world. Eyelids are, well, lids for your eyes, and they work great without you even thinking about it. But they are no match for flying objects, big or small, which can result in a *shiner* (that's slang for black eye) or pieces of stuff floating around in there. Blink! Blink!

SPECIAL HELP in examining eyes

Examining your own eye: Look in a mirror while pulling up your upper lid and pulling down your lower lid. Do you see anything?

Examining someone else's eye: Pull the lower lid down and have the person look up. Do you see anything? Pull up the upper lid and have the person look down. Anything there?

Black Eye

GET HELP!

TELL a grown-up NOW to TAKE you to the emergency room or to CALL 9-1-1 NOW (if you are alone, CALL 9-1-1 NOW) if you have been hit very hard in the head or eye area and are having severe pain, bleeding from the eyes or nose, or blurry or double vision.

TELL a grown-up NOW and GO to a doctor NOW if you have sustained a hard blow to the eye area. There could be injury to your skull bones, brain, or vision — especially if you were hit hard. **Apply an ice pack until you arrive at the doctor's office.**

TELL a grown-up NOW and GO to a doctor TODAY if there is increasing redness, pain, drainage, or bleeding, or if you have changes in your vision.

Did I mention ... PREVENTION?

Be wise about your eyes

* **Be alert.** Keep your attention focused on whatever you are doing. Always keep your eye on the ball!
* **Wear protective eyewear.** Goggles are a good idea if you are working on projects that throw out debris (such as woodworking), mowing lawns, or doing cleanup projects. If you are working on projects at home or in school that require substances that could sting or damage your eyes, definitely goggle up!
* **Polycarbonate lenses.** If you wear glasses, polycarbonate lenses are shatter-proof and durable. They'll help you keep your peepers safe!

Chemical Splash

If a chemical (for example, laundry detergent or garden fertilizer) gets splashed into your eye, it can cause a serious burn injury. See CHEMICAL BURNS, pages 59–60.

WHAT TO EXPECT

A painful thump to the eye area. Something's out of control. Is it you?

Swelling and bruising around the eye. Puffy, then black and blue!

Discomfort. A general aching, bruised sensation.

WHAT TO DO
THE GOOD-BYE BLACK-EYE CURE

This is for any minor shiner. Your body, of course, is going to do the repair and cleanup work, but you can certainly do your best to help it along.

You'll need: Ice pack or washcloth (for the first two days), warm washcloth (for the third day and beyond).

1. A black eye should be iced immediately to reduce the swelling and bruising. (Ice helps the blood vessels shrink and reduces the amount of bleeding under the skin.)

2. **First two days:** Apply an ice pack or washcloth *very gently* three or four times a day for 10 to 15 minutes each time. Don't blow your nose, as that could cause more bleeding. A grown-up might give you something for the pain. *Don't take or give any medications by yourself.*

3. **Third day and beyond:** Apply the warm washcloth to the eye area three to four times a day, until the area is healed. This increases the circulation to the area and helps with dead-cell cleanup.

SPECIAL HELP for a black eye at bedtime

Reducing the swelling and bleeding is important during the first few minutes and hours in the life of a black eye. It's harder to bleed (and swell) if the injury is uphill, so sleep with your head propped up on pillows and don't sleep on the injured side.

Sleep with your head propped up when you have a (new) black eye.

Foreign Object

WHAT TO EXPECT

Scratchy, burning, teary, sensitive-to-light sensation. This depends on what's stuck in there … an eyelash or a golf ball!

Pain. If it is something very large or irritating, or if something is actually poking into the eyeball, you'll feel pain, rather than irritation.

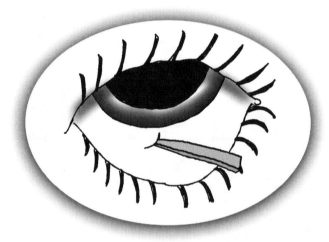

Bandage over both eyes

OR

Cup over eye with small bandage over other eye

GET HELP!

**TELL a grown-up NOW
to TAKE you to the emergency room
or to CALL 9-1-1 NOW
(if you are alone, call 9-1-1 NOW)**
if an object, large or small, is not floating on the clear film of the eye but is **stuck into the eyeball. Cover both eyes gently to prevent movement that could cause further injury. If the object is large, tape a cup over the eye so the object cannot be pushed farther in.**

**TELL a grown-up NOW and
GO to a doctor TODAY**

☞ if the eye remains scratchy, teary, and uncomfortable. There may be a scratch on the *cornea* (the clear front covering of the eyeball) or something too small to see in your eye.

☞ if you have any of these signs of infection over the next few days: increased pain, redness, or swelling; any streaking or milky, stinking drainage (pus); or fever.

WHAT TO DO

Objective: To safely remove small foreign objects from the eye — dirt, sand, eyelashes (or whatever is floating around in there that shouldn't be!).

Warning: Eyes should never be treated with anything but clean water or sterile saline solution unless directly by a doctor.

You'll need: Soap and water, small clean cup, mirror, cotton swab.

1. **Don't rub your eye,** as this will just scratch it. Wash your hands with warm water and soap — you don't want to introduce any more FOs (**f**oreign **o**bjects) in there such as germs or dirt.

2. **Rinse** your eye by tilting your head to the problem side. Using the clean cup, gently run clean, warm water from the inner part of the eye to the outer part of the eye. Do this several times.

3. If you still feel the object is in there after rinsing, use the mirror to **examine** your eye. (See Special Help, page 81.)

4. If you see a small object floating on the clear film of the eye, take a moist cotton swab (Q-tip) or the corner of a soft cloth and lightly touch the object. It should come out easily. Rinse the eye again with warm, clean water.

5. If you don't see anything, but your eye still feels a little scratchy, teary, and uncomfortable, and it looks red, you are experiencing the normal result of having had something irritating in your eye. It should be a mild feeling and go away in a few minutes.

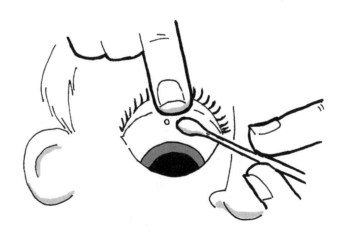

HOW TO REMOVE A FLOATER FROM YOUR EYE

You are now wise to your eyes. Nice work!

FROZEN TOES & OTHER COLD TROUBLES

Frostnip, Frostbite & Mild Hypothermia

Everybody knows Jack Frost. He's that happy cold-weather fellow who likes to nip at your nose and toes, but what he looks like nobody knows! That "pins and needles" feeling that you get when you are out in the cold is his calling card. If you take care of the early nip, you won't get a bite, *frostbite*, that is, which means — and this is true — ice crystals are starting to form in your skin tissues.

BRRR!

Frostnip and Frostbite

GET HELP!
FROSTBITE*

TELL a grown-up NOW to TAKE you to the emergency room or to CALL 9-1-1 NOW (if you are alone, call 9-1-1 NOW) if you think you have suffered frostbite.

☞ **DON'T use the frostbitten part of your body.**

☞ **DON'T rub the skin (the ice crystals in the tissues will act like slivers).**

☞ **DON'T thaw out the area if there is any danger of it refreezing (this would cause more damage than if it was left frozen).**

☞ **DON'T use hot water, hot-water bottles, heating lamps, heating pads, campfires, or car heaters to thaw. They are too hot!**

*If you suspect hypothermia, see page 92.

Q & Ask the Nurse

Q: **Where on your body are you most likely to suffer frostbite?**

A: You can probably make some pretty good guesses just by remembering where you felt the coldest on a bitter cold day. Here is a list, beginning with the most common spots that don't thrill to the chill: fingertips, toes, earlobes, tip of the nose, cheeks, and any other exposed skin.

Did I mention ... PREVENTION?

Scold the cold!

In winter weather and in springtime when days are warm but evenings turn cold, please take these precautions:

✳ **Cover up.** Dress in layers — long underwear, then turtleneck, a sweater, and finish off with a wind- and water-resistant coat. You trap lots of air this way and keep the warmest layers for yourself! So put 'em all on!

✳ **Wear a hat.** You lose most of your heat off the top of your head. In really cold weather, wear a hat that covers up everything *but* your nostrils and eyes.

✳ **Protect hands and feet.** Mittens are better than gloves — your fingers can share the heat — and wool or polypropylene socks are better than cotton. Keep the layers next to your skin dry because moisture *wicks* (draws) heat away from your body.

✳ **Follow the safety rules of the recreational activity you are involved in.** Know the rules for cold-weather safety. It could save your ... toes ... your nose ... or your life!

✳ **Do buddy checks.** Check out your friends for red, chilled-looking spots on their skin *(frostnip),* and ask them to do the same for you.

✳ **Consider the wind-chill factor.** *Wind chill* means that the actual temperature your body experiences is lower than the thermometer says, when wind is present.

✳ **Drink up.** Not only does hot cocoa taste good and warm you up, but liquids of any kind prevent dehydration that can make cold injuries more likely. So have a cup. Or two!

✳ **Don't lick (ick!) or touch cold metal with your bare hands.** You'll get the super freeze and stick! *Eek!*

✳ **Be nature's assistant.** Don't ignore skin changes and sensations. It's your body talking, so listen up!

✳ **Know (and tell others) that nicotine and alcohol are even more dangerous in cold-weather situations.** They reduce blood circulation and change your *metabolism* (how your body makes energy), which make them especially dangerous in the cold.

WHAT TO EXPECT

Skin changes. At first nip, the skin will be bright pink and then it becomes very red and slightly swollen. If frostbite sets in, the skin will appear white and sometimes there will be blisters. Now your skin is really mad!

Discomfort. With frostnip, there is a "pins and needles" feeling and an aching sensation. With frostbite, the discomfort will fade and the area will become numb and feel hard like wax.

Signs of hypothermia (possibly). See page 92.

WHAT TO DO

If it's frostbite, see GET HELP!, page 87.

Cover up the chilled part. Put your hands or fingers in your armpits (or someone else's!), cover your cheeks and nose with your hands, pull a hat over your ears. Use anything to protect the area from any more cold. Enough is enough!

Go to a warm place. Your house, tent, or cave. Just go!

Remove any wet clothing. It is just sucking the heat out of you, and you don't have any to spare!

Do a warm soak. Using warm water — *not* hot water — soak the area for 10 to 15 minutes. If you can't soak the area (it's your nose, for example … *blub, blub, blub),* apply a warm, moist cloth instead.

I wouldn't do that if I were you…

 Check It Out!

No licking!

Place a damp piece of cloth on a piece of frozen metal, such as metal stair rails or a metal rack in your freezer. What happens? The moisture on the cloth is quick-frozen by the supercold metal, causing it to stick to the metal. Now, try to pull off the cloth. See what happens? A bit of the cloth is frozen fast and stays behind. Now how do you think your tongue would feel after that! *Youch!*

Frostbite show & tell

You'll need: Small piece of frozen steak-like meat, freezer, magnifying glass.

1. Remove the meat from the freezer and examine it closely with the magnifying glass. What do you notice?

2. Now let the meat thaw very slightly and massage it, imagining that it is your skin and the tissues beneath it. What do you think would happen to it?

3. Let the meat thaw and then refreeze it before examining it again. What do you notice this time that differs from the first freeze?

So, using your observation skills — a key ingredient to good first aid — you probably noticed miniature ice crystals in the frozen meat in step 1. That's just like what happens to frozen skin and tissue.

When you massaged the meat in step 2, you might have guessed correctly that the ice crystals would slice the tissue like small slivers. That's gotta hurt!

When you examined the refrozen meat in step 3, did you see how much larger the ice crystals were? That indicates that the skin and tissues would become even more damaged if you were to refreeze a frostbitten area.

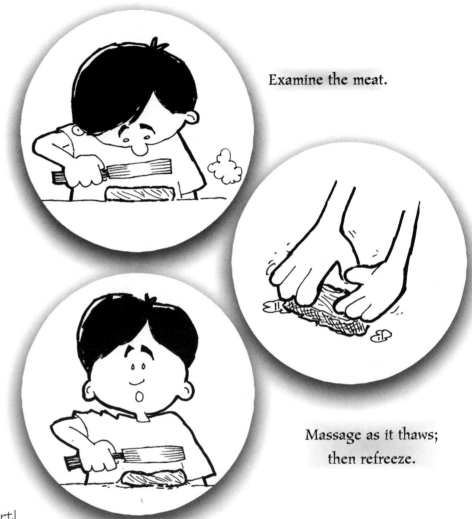

Examine the meat.

Massage as it thaws; then refreeze.

Hmmm! What do you notice now?

Check It Out!

It's the pits!

Forget hot pads, you have hot pits (armpits, that is!).

You'll need: Cool water, 1 mitten, your hands (both, please), your armpits (hey, you don't even have to get up to get those ...).

1. Place your hands in the cool water for a minute or two. Put a mitten on one hand and leave the other hand bare. Now tuck your *bare* hand into your armpit. Which hand is warmer?

Pity, isn't it?

2. Now tuck the mitten-covered hand *and* the bare hand into each of your armpits. Which hand is warmer?

Step 1: The one in the pit wins!

Step 2: The bare hand still wins, because skin to skin contact transfers heat better.

(P.S. Check out THE NAKED TRUTH on page 93.)

Q & Ask the Nurse

The heat-leak quiz

Q: **How many different ways does your body lose heat?**

A. *Five.* (1) Through contact with something cold, (2) air moving across our bodies, (3) sweating, (4) breathing, and (5) invisible heat-wave loss.

B. *Three.* (1) By panting like a dog, (2) flapping your ears like an elephant, and (3) sweating.

C. *Two.* (1) By sweating, and (2) by wearing wet clothes.

D. *None.* Your body doesn't lose heat, it makes it.

See below for the answer. How'd you do?

A: **B.** Hah! Just kidding! It's **A.** (We don't pant like a dog — or fetch like one either!)

Mild Hypothermia

Hypothermia, the unwanted lowering of your body temperature, can happen

❄ in really cold and snowy weather,

❄ to people who are, for example, stranded in cold water after falling off a boat,

❄ or to people who are inadequately dressed and exposed for a long period of time to wet, windy, or cold weather.

GET HELP!

TELL a grown-up NOW to TAKE you to the emergency room or to CALL 9-1-1 NOW (if you are alone, CALL 9-1-1 NOW) if someone has symptoms such as these, indicating a more serious stage of hypothermia:

☞ extreme clumsiness

☞ confused thoughts

☞ feeling very sleepy

☞ weak or losing consciousness

☞ no longer shivering

☞ very slow breathing

Keep the person warm on the way.

You feel cold. No kidding!

Shivering. When you shiver, your muscles move; muscles in motion create heat. Your body is trying to warm up!

Clumsy hands. No knives, please!

Faster breathing and heart rate. Your body's way of bringing in more oxygen.

Lower core body temperature (not skin temperature) from above 95°F/35°C to below 98.6°F/37°C.

The Kids' Guide to First Aid

WHAT TO DO

Get someplace warm. Anywhere out of the wind — a house, tent, or cave! Cover your head and be sure there is something between you and the cold ground — even branches will help.

Cover up. Put it all on, baby, whatever you've got. Blankets, underwear, scarves, and more please!

Drink up. The good warm stuff like hot chocolate and tea.

Check for frostnip or frostbite. See page 89.

Get moving. Physical activity revs up the body's furnace. Jump in place, make windmills with your arms (without accidentally punching anybody in the nose!).

Be supportive. There's nothing like the calm voice and the *warm* and helpful hands of a friend.

FIRST-AID TRICKS

The Naked Truth

Bodies are generous with their heat and share it best, well, cheek to cheek. Put cold skin next to warm skin — fingers go in armpits, toes, *uh,* in someone else's armpits (unless you can fold yourself up to put them in your own!), and cover your nose with warm hands. A person who is suffering from *severe* hypothermia can be rescued by stripping the person of his clothes (yup, that's naked) and sandwiching him between two other stripped-down people (yup, they're naked, too). In emergencies, you gotta do what you gotta do. And that's the Naked Truth!

 Whether you get a nip from Jack Frost or get super chilled, you know just what to do. Pass it on. You're good at this!

POISON IVY, OAK & SUMAC
BOY, DOES THAT ITCH!

Sure, you've itched before. No big deal, right? That is until you have a run-in with some poison ivy, oak, or sumac. Then you *really* know what itching is! Although some people never develop sensitivity — how lucky is that? — most of us will somehow manage to crush a stem or leaf and spend the next 10 days a-scratchin' and a-scratchin' some more!

poison ivy

poison oak

poison sumac

Leaves of three, let them be.

94

WHAT TO EXPECT

The symptoms usually last about 10 days to two weeks and are generally at their worst by the fifth day.

Red, pimply rash. It shows up a half day to two days after exposure.

Itching. Boy, howdy, some serious itching!

Blisters. These appear after a couple of days, but don't worry. They aren't contagious! (You can't spread the itching to anyone else except by spreading the resin.)

GET HELP!

TELL a grown-up NOW and GO to a doctor TODAY

☞ if you have symptoms of a severe reaction (they'll appear within just a few hours): eyes swell shut, you are extremely uncomfortable, and there is so much itching and oozing that your clothes stick to you.

☞ if the resin has caused a reaction on your face, genitals (your private parts), or in your eyes.

☞ if you have any of these signs of infection over the next few days: increased pain, redness, or swelling; any streaking or milky, stinking drainage (pus); or fever.

Use a hose — not a tub!

WHAT TO DO

Remove all resin from your body and clothes. See page 97.

Don't pop the blisters. They are small and prevent infection if left undisturbed. You may cover them with a clean gauze pad or a Band-Aid if there is a particularly troublesome spot.

Try not to scratch. Boy, that *will* be hard! Keep your hands clean in case you scratch in your sleep! Be as patient as you can, even though life with a big itch is a big drag!

Pain medication. A grown-up might give you some medication to help reduce your skin's reaction to the resin. *Don't take or give any medications by yourself.*

Did I mention ... PREVENTION?

Poisonous plant proofing

✳ **Be a nature investigator.** These plants are young and especially tender in the spring, so they will break more easily and — *eek!* — leak! So, know what these plants look like — and avoid them! (See page 94.)

✳ **Cover up.** Wear long-sleeved clothes if you are going out bushwhacking!

✳ **Don't burn these plants.** The plant oils are released into the air in the form of tiny droplets, landing on your skin and inside your nose and throat. Wouldn't want to try to scratch in there!

✳ **Wash even if you are not sure it was a poisonous plant.** Better safe than sorry!

✳ **Wash Fido, too.** Pets can get the resin on their fur and then when you pet them, guess where the resin lands? Nothing a good bath with lots of soap and water won't cure. Wearing rubber gloves when you're scrubbin' is a good idea, too!

WHAT TO DO

OPERATION RESIN REMOVAL

Objective: To remove the resin immediately from the skin in order to reduce or prevent a reaction to the poisonous plant.

You'll need: *Running* water (alcohol wipes or rubbing alcohol and cotton balls as an alternative), soap.

1. *Immediately* — within 10 minutes is best — wash off the exposed areas with *running* water and soap. (It must be running water, as water in a sink would collect the resin and you'd be re-exposed by dipping into it.) *Don't use a washcloth to wash off the resin. It will only spread the resin over your body.* No water? In a pinch, you can use alcohol wipes or rubbing alcohol and cotton balls to break down the resin.

2. Wash all clothes, shoes, and any objects that came in contact with the resin to prevent spreading it.

☑ Check It Out!   Resin lesson

You'll need: Water, clear glass, cooking oil (olive, corn, safflower, etc.), fork, liquid soap.

Resin is like oil, and oils don't mix with or dissolve in water. Pour a small amount of water into the glass. Then, pour a small amount of the oil into the glass. See how the oil sits on top of the water without blending? Now try mixing them together as if you were beating eggs. They still don't mix. And how about if you add soap? It just drops through the oil into the water. Like resin, that oil just wants to keep hanging around.

You can see why it's important to use running water to wash off poisonous plant resin!

Are You Wishing to Stop the Itching?

The itching drives some people crazy, but there are lots of remedies to help you out.

- Apply an ICE PACK or a damp cloth to the itchy spots, or place the itchy area under cold running water. While you are still damp, stand in front of a fan to help dry up the skin.

- CALAMINE LOTION also helps dry up the blisters and reduce the itching. Stop using it once the blisters dry up, so the skin doesn't crack.

- HYDROCORTISONE CREAM applied to the super-itchy spots can help, or you can use the juice or gel from an ALOE VERA plant (see SPECIAL HELP FOR BURNS, page 53).

- A SOOTHING BATH. Just as for a sunburn, take a bath with ½ cup (125 ml) of baking soda or a packet of Aveeno colloidal oatmeal. If you only have regular oatmeal, you can still benefit from tubbing in it (just fill a woman's stocking with regular (not instant) oatmeal, tie the top, and toss it into the tub with you). Weird, but nice!

 GOOD FOR YOU! IT'S COOL THAT YOU KNOW WHAT TO DO!

POISONING
Don't Swallow That!

Poisonous substances — naturally occurring and man-made — are dangerous and deadly to your body if you eat them, inhale them, or absorb them. So don't! Little kids are the ones most at risk. To them, gasoline looks like juice, medicine like candy, and beautiful wild berries like a tasty snack. And those little kids are fast! They can take a gulp of something dangerous while you turn away for just a second. Poisons cause your body to suffer injury to tissues, nerves, organs, and your blood, impairing your body's ability to carry oxygen, which is, as you know, kind of hard to live without!

GET HELP!

TELL a grown-up NOW to CALL the Poison Control Center, CALL 9-1-1, or GO to an emergency room NOW (if you are alone, CALL 9-1-1 NOW) if you suspect or know someone has been exposed to a poisonous substance.

Mr. Yuk and the National Capital Poison Center's poison warning symbol

Post your local Poison Control Center's telephone number by your phone!

It's listed with other emergency numbers at the front of the phone book.

(See Make-Your-Own Emergency Number Checklist, page 11)

✴ **Be a First-Aid Star:** Know the poison's name, how much, and how long ago the person was exposed to it and be able to explain the person's symptoms.

There are other ways to be poisoned besides swallowing a poisonous substance:

🕷 **For poisonous spider bites,** see pages 29–31

〰 **For poisonous snakebites,** see pages 36–38

〰 **For jellyfish bites,** see pages 17–19

🍃 **For poison ivy, oak, and sumac,** see pages 94–98

Did I mention ... PREVENTION?
Be on "poison patrol"

Get Mr. Yuk stickers from your local Poison Control Center or labels from the National Capital Poison Center. Teach your younger siblings what this sticker means, and ask a grown-up if you can place the stickers on the items on the list below.

Beware! Poison! Here is a list of things that are poisonous, or can be poisonous under certain conditions. Are you surprised to see some of these things on this list?

* **Chemicals** (gasoline, garden fertilizer, bleach, paint, paint thinner)
* **Mushrooms** (some)
* **Plants,** including seeds, leaves, flowers, and berries (some)
* **Medicines** (too much or the wrong ones, or taking someone else's)
* **Make-up**
* **Shellfish,** harvested during a red tide
* **Car exhaust fumes**
* **Food,** improperly stored or prepared
* **Home-canned food,** if the canning jar has a bulging lid
* **Vitamins with A, D, E, and K, and/or iron.** Large doses of any of these can harm you.
* **Nail polish and remover**
* **Dishwasher soap**

Want to learn more about poison prevention? Visit the National Capital Poison Center website at **<www.poison.org>**.

For more on Mr. Yuk, visit him at **<www.poison.org/mrYuk.htm>**.

Think poison if someone is complaining of illness and there is evidence of a poisonous substance nearby. For example:

☞ Someone has eaten an unknown berry and becomes sick to his stomach and throws up.

☞ Someone has burns around her mouth and lips, and her breath smells like a chemical (perhaps there is paint thinner nearby?).

☞ Someone is having trouble breathing and feels sleepy or confused after being in a garage while a car was running.

☞ There is an open bottle of medication that was not prescribed for the person who took it, and now he is light-headed or sick to his stomach.

Poisonings often imitate other illnesses, like a stroke or a diabetic reaction. Now when someone becomes ill suddenly and there's evidence of poisoning, you can get help immediately. There are many possibilities, so keep your eyes, your ears, and your nose open, especially when little kids are around!

Diarrhea, nausea, vomiting, and stomach pain _could_ signal food poisoning. Most people experience symptoms for a day or so and then improve. Severe cases involve worsening of symptoms and bloody diarrhea. If bloody, go to a doctor today.

☑ Check It Out!
Food gone bad

You'll need: 3 pieces of bread, 3 plastic sandwich bags, refrigerator with freezer (That's it. The bacteria do the rest — and they arrive uninvited!).

Place one piece of bread in each sandwich bag. Store one at room temperature, one in the refrigerator, and one in the freezer. Which one do you think is going to become moldy first? Check on each piece during the next two weeks. Were you right? I know which one I would put in the toaster …

WHEN BREAD GOES BAD

The Kids' Guide to First Aid

WHAT TO DO

Get help from a grown-up. Be sure the person is in a safe and comfortable place and is no longer in danger of being exposed to the dangerous substance. Offer your coat or a blanket and let the person know you are going to get a grown-up and will be right back.

Be reassuring. Think about how bad you felt when you had the flu and double it!

Know why bacteria are so good at math?

'Cause we can multiply so fast! HA HA!

 SPECIAL HELP *for safe eating*

Bacteria that cause illnesses to humans are everywhere — in food and water, and living on our skin and in our intestines (that's why you wash your hands before eating). But not all bacteria are the same, and what makes people sick may be just fine for a bird or your cat. To protect yourself from getting food poisoning, prepare, cook, and store food properly.

Food rules to follow:

- **Eat meats well done** — not pink or red.

- **Eat cold foods cold** (especially those with eggs, meat, dairy, or mayonnaise in them).

- **Eat hot foods hot.**

- **Wash fresh fruits and vegetables before eating.**

- **Make sure it's fresh** — it shouldn't stink or have grown green hair!

- **If you aren't sure if it's safe to eat some-thing, don't eat it.**

- **Wash your hands before and after preparing food.**

Good for you for learning about poison prevention. It sure is important stuff!

SPLINTERS

How'd a Tree Get Under There?

Who would have thought that such a little thing as a splinter (also called a *sliver*) could be so annoying? There you are harmlessly frolicking about and — ping! — a sliver of wood has just zipped under your skin.

GET HELP!

TELL a grown-up NOW and GO to a doctor TODAY if you have any of these signs of infection over the next few days: increased pain, redness, or swelling; any streaking or milky, stinking drainage (pus); or fever.

Did I mention ...
PREVENTION?

Be sliver-less so you'll quiver less!

* **Wear shoes and gloves at all times!** Just kidding, at least about wearing them at *all* times. But hauling wood? Wear gloves. Playing on a wood surface? Then, shoes are the best friends of all!

* **Don't slide your hand (or bottom!) down wooden stair rails.** Otherwise, a soon-to-be splinter might become an itty-bitty spear. Gotcha!

WHAT TO EXPECT

A splinter! Small or large, it may be partly exposed or buried deeper so nothing sticks out.

Discomfort. Your body's way of getting your attention! It may take a day or two before you are even aware that a splinter is there.

Mild redness and swelling. This is your body's natural reaction to something foreign moving in. It is trying to protect you against infection and eject the little bugger at the same time!

WHAT TO DO
LEAVE IT BE ... OR SET IT FREE?

Here are some jingles to help you remember what to do.

If it's tiny, it'll be fine-y.

Just let these little guys be. Your body will work the sliver out. Put a dab of antibiotic ointment over the top, keep the area clean, and "let your bod do its job!"

Small or large, but with a tail,
To the SPLINTER STATION sail!

Please see OPERATION SPLINTER STATION on page 107. Can't get to a SPLINTER STATION? Squeeze around the splinter entrance to give the area a *blood wash.* Hey, that's not gross! It helps rinse out the wood and bring resources to heal and fight infection. So, give it a squeeze, please!

If it's super large and very deep,
Go to a grown-up without a peep.

If it will require lots of digging around, it's better to have a doctor do it under sterile conditions. Tell a grown-up you've got a humdinger!

FIRST-AID TRICKS
S. O. S. — Soak Out Splinters

A splinter that is below the skin can be encouraged to surface on its own with a good soak in warm water. After soaking it for about 10 minutes, rub the skin away from the splinter on each side with a washcloth and see if that brings it to the surface. Remove as directed in OPERATION SPLINTER STATION, page 107. If it's still hiding, wait a day or two and try again.

TINY

SMALL TO LARGE, BUT TWEEZER-ABLE

LARGE AND DEEP

I "wood" go see a doctor.

WHAT TO DO

Location, location, location. Locate your SPLINTER STATION (bathrooms and kitchens are good places) where there is:

- ☞ a good light,
- ☞ a good place to sit down (toilets or chairs),
- ☞ warm water and soap for washing.

Splinters of all kinds are welcomed here and will be treated in the order received. So no pushing and shoving, please!

You'll need: Soap and water, magnifying glass (optional), tweezers, alcohol wipes (or rubbing alcohol and cotton balls), sewing needle, antibiotic ointment, Band-Aid.

1. Upon arrival at the Station, wash your hands and the area around the splinter. Pesky germs are always looking for a chance to sneak in!

2. Check out the sliver. Use the magnifying glass and look at it under good light to see what you've got!

3. Clean the tweezers with an alcohol wipe and don't touch the ends once they are cleaned. Grasp the exposed piece of the splinter and pull it out in the same direction it entered.

4. Can't quite reach it? Clean the needle with an alcohol wipe. Then use the needle to *gently* scrape away the surrounding skin until the tweezers can grasp the splinter and pull it out.

5. Put on a dab of antibiotic ointment, followed by a Band-Aid. Keep the area clean until the skin is healed.

OPERATION

SPLINTER STATION

GOOD LIGHT

SOAP

WATER

MAGNIFYING GLASS

TWEEZERS

ALCOHOL WIPES (OR RUBBING ALCOHOL & COTTON BALLS)

SEWING NEEDLE

BAND-AIDS

ANTIBIOTIC OINTMENT

Now splinters won't scare you because you have learned what to do. Keep up the good work!

SPRAINS & STRAINS
TWIST & SHOUT!

There you are, just minding your own business, running along and then *wham!* Your foot catches on a root and the next thing you know, you are facedown with dirt on your lip and one sore ankle. Or, maybe, your knee got twisted or a finger got some encouragement to bend the wrong way. Don't you hate it when that happens? Sprains and strains are common, especially in sports, and are usually nothing serious. If it is more serious, don't worry, you'll know it: It'll throb like a bass drum and puff up like a sausage. Twist and shout!

Did I mention ... PREVENTION?
Avoiding the herky-jerkies

✱ **Warm up those muscles!** Before starting a sports activity, jog in place, stretch, and walk briskly (pages 115–116). Get into the sport gradually over a few minutes, giving your muscles a chance to get a good supply of blood.

✱ **Cool down after.** Stretching or light walking helps keep the muscles from shortening and trapping the by-products of exercise (*lactic acid*) in the tissue, causing stiffness.

✱ **Wear good shoes.** Shoes should hold your feet firmly and prevent your ankles from rocking back and forth. Sport shoes should offer maximum cushioning, sidewall support, and good traction, so you stop when your feet do!

✱ **No pain = no sprain or strain!** You've probably heard the saying, "No pain, no gain." That's old news (and wrong!), my friend. Trying your best should never be accompanied by pain. If it hurts, stop and give it a rest — or risk being out of the game for a long time!

✱ **Use good sports equipment and follow the rules.** Both of these things prevent accidents — to you or someone else!

✱ **Ice it anyway.** Any joint or muscle that's sore after a workout can benefit from applying an ice pack for 15 minutes. This reduces the likelihood of swelling.

Q: **How old do I have to be to snow-board or surf?**

A: Play sports that your body is ready for. Does that mean waiting until you are 30 before you do the pipeline? No, but in any sport, be certain your body has developed the muscles and coordination necessary for safe participation. Some of this comes with age and development — not skill! Ask a grown-up like a doctor or coach for some guidance. And don't worry — you'll be hot-doggin' it before you know it!

GET HELP!

Tell a grown-up NOW and GO to a doctor NOW if you feel or hear a popping sound or there is severe pain and/or disability at the time of the injury. Apply an ice pack to the injured area *immediately* and keep the injured part elevated and immobile on the way to the doctor.

TELL a grown-up NOW and GO to a doctor TODAY if any minor injury starts to become more painful and swollen, or you have a fever (because what was nothin' is now somethin'!).

"...and now all the other kids call me "Bruise Willis!"

WHAT TO EXPECT

These all depend on the extent of the injury.

Pain. You can't pull a muscle or overstretch a ligament without the message going to your brain. It sounds something like this, *"Aaaaaaaagh!"*

Tender to the touch. So quit touching it!

Swelling. Some fluid seeps in from the surrounding tissue and *poof!* — you've got yourself a sausage finger or balloon knee.

Bruising. Small blood vessels might break from the tension, leaking blood under the skin.

Less ROM (Range **o**f **M**otion**).** Because of discomfort or other problems like swelling or a tear, you might not be able to move the area fully at least for a minute or two. My advice? Don't try — just give it a rest.

WHAT TO DO

Offer comfort to the injured person. A grown-up might give you something for the pain. *Don't take or give any medications by yourself.* Then, R.I.C.E. it!

R.I.C.E. IT!

R.I.C.E. is an important technique for the management of muscle and joint injuries. It applies to serious injuries, as well as to minor ones that kids can handle, like a sore finger or an aching knee.

☞ **R = Rest.** Stop and rest the area *as soon as it hurts.* If the discomfort stops after a brief rest, gently rotate and flex the area to see if there is any remaining discomfort; if not, then you are good to go. If it still hurts, it's time to I.C.E. it (read on). But keep resting and — yup — that could take a few days or even more!

☞ **I = Ice.** *Remember: No ice applied directly onto your skin.* Ice is essential for minor twists and turns that don't stop hurting after a brief rest. For serious sprains and strains, it should be applied immediately, pronto, stat! — *even if you are going to seek medical help.* Icing *really* makes a difference. Apply an ice pack or use a bag of frozen peas, a chilled can of soda, or, if the injury is large, such as your whole foot, a bucket of ice water — anything to get those blood vessels to *constrict* (shrink) and not set off a four-bell alarm.

☞ **C = Compress.** This means wrapping firmly, but not tightly, the injured area in an elastic bandage. The pressure encourages the stray fluid to get back into the vessels where it belongs and circulate. Don't be lazy: Do this even with minor strains. It reduces the chance of swelling and supports the injured area. Apply ice right on top of the bandage!

☞ **E = Elevate.** Raise the injured area above your heart right away. Do this also at night. Gravity helps drain the excess fluid from the tissues.

15-3-3 Ice Chart

✔ 15 minutes of ice
✔ every 1–3 hours while awake
✔ for 3 days (or until swelling is gone).

How's My Hurt?

ICE CHART	Day 1	Day 2	Day 3
8 a.m.	✔		
9		✔	
10	✔		
11			
12 NOON			
1 p.m.	✔		
2			
3			
4	✔		
5			
6			
7	✔		
8			

Practice Wrapping It Up

FIRST-AID TRICKS

Use an elastic bandage to practice wrapping some of the more common injuries on yourself, a friend, or a stuffed animal.

IMPORTANT TIPS!

✱ Don't get over-energetic and put a bandage on too tight. Tighter is not better! It could cause more pain, numbness, and swelling. Duh, weren't you trying to get rid of those? So loosen up!

✱ Wrapping know-how:
  • begin wrapping at the farthest point from your heart;
  • wrap gently;
  • wrap from slightly below to slightly above the injury.

✱ Use a *splint* (to keep the injured part immobile) made of rolled-up newspaper or two rulers, for example, secured with shoelaces or strips of cloth (see page 30).

gauze

FINGER BANDAGE

ANKLE WRAP

"BUDDY TAPING" OF TOES

Make-Your-Own Arm Sling

A sling allows you to elevate a hand or wrist and still be mobile.

YOU'LL NEED: A piece of lightweight cloth (42" x 42"/ 105 x 105 cm*), measuring tape or ruler, pencil, scissors (to cut fabric), safety pin (to fasten the sling).

TO USE ON AN INJURED ARM:

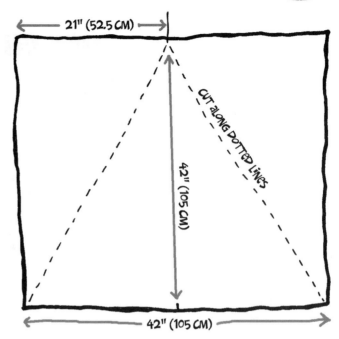

21" (52.5 CM)

42" (105 CM)

CUT ALONG DOTTED LINES

42" (105 CM)

MAKE A SLING TO KEEP IN YOUR FIRST-AID KIT

injured arm

uninjured arm

1. Place one end of the triangle over the shoulder of the *uninjured* side. The sling base and the other end of the triangle should be hanging down over the chest and *under* the injured arm.

2. Fold the injured arm across the chest, keeping the fingers higher than the elbow.

*Note: In a pinch, use a long-sleeved shirt (tie the sleeves around the neck and use the body of the shirt as the sling) or two bandannas tied together.

3. Take the other end of the triangle and tie it at the back of the neck in a knot (raise the injured arm up a little higher since the knot will slacken after it is tied). Keep the fingers exposed.

4. Secure the safety pin in front of the elbow. Want to go totally professional? Roll up a washcloth and curve your hand in its normal functional position lightly around the cloth. Wow! Nice job!

Safety pin

DID YOU KNOW...

that sprains are different from strains? *Strains* involve muscles and tendons that get overworked, overstretched, or injured. They are usually less serious than sprains. *Sprains* involve torn *ligaments* (the fibrous bands that connect bones at joints). Ligaments have a poor blood supply, and that means they often take longer to heal. So don't *strain* yourself or you're more likely to *sprain* yourself!

SPECIAL HELP for speeding the healing

If there is no more swelling *after two days*, apply warmth to speed up the healing. Use either a heating pad (with grown-up supervision), a warm (not hot) water bottle, or a soak in the tub. The heat improves circulation to the area by *dilating* (opening up) the blood vessels. That means more cleanup because more of the "Home Team" is working on it!

Warm-up stretches

Ankles: Rotate each ankle 10 times in one direction and 10 in the other.

Calves: Lean against a wall with one foot closer to the wall than the other. Press down through the heel in the foot farthest from the wall. Repeat with the other leg.

Hamstrings (back of thigh): Sit on the ground, one leg stretched out in front of you, the other bent with your foot tucked close to your groin. Lean over slowly and try to touch your abdomen to the knee of the straight leg. Switch legs.

Sprains & Strains

Lower back: Lie flat on your back with both knees bent. Raise one knee to your chest and, with both hands, gently pull it toward your shoulder. Repeat with the other leg.

Chest and upper body: Place your hands behind your head and clasp your fingers together. Push your elbows back while breathing in deeply several times.

Neck: While sitting or standing, tilt your head to the side toward your shoulder. Then gently stretch your arm (on the opposite side) to the floor. Repeat on other side. Finish with a few chin-to-chest stretches.

The Kids' Guide to First Aid

Gravity to the rescue!

Ever wonder why you are always told to raise the injured area above your heart to prevent swelling or to slow bleeding. See for yourself — the wonders of gravity, your own first-aid tool that is always with you!

You'll need: Marker, 2 balloons, water, drinking straw, 2 rubber bands.

1. Draw a heart on one balloon. Fill it up with water. Place one end of the straw into the neck of the balloon and twist the rubber band tightly around it. You now have a heart, ready to pump.

2. Draw a foot and an ankle on the second balloon. Without spilling the water in the heart balloon, slide the free end of the straw into the foot balloon. Secure it by twisting on the other rubber band. You now have a healthy foot and ankle.

3. Oops! You just tripped and injured your ankle and foot. With the fluid in the heart balloon, tip the ankle balloon toward the ground (that's where your feet usually are, after all). See how the fluid fills up the injured ankle balloon so that it bulges? Your real foot and ankle tissues would swell up even more, because the heart is a pump, so it's constantly pushing blood and fluid down there.

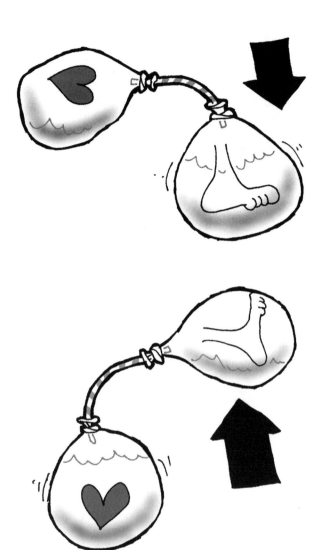

4. Now, elevate the ankle balloon above the heart balloon, like a good first-aid kid would do. See how all the fluid runs into the heart balloon where it can be recirculated and eliminated? Gravity to the rescue! (The heart won't bulge or become swollen like a balloon because it's always pumping.)

5. Now, add some compression. Lower the ankle balloon to let it fill. Then, elevate the ankle balloon above the heart balloon and gently squeeze the ankle (as if you had applied a bandage). See how the fluid squirts out faster? If you compress the ankle balloon while it is elevated above the heart balloon, the liquid leaves the injury even faster.

✳ NICE WORK! YOU WILL BE A FRIEND INDEED WITH THIS FIRST-AID KNOW-HOW!

TEETH
What's Right for Your Pearly Whites

Y ou get two sets of teeth, which is a pretty cool thing when you think about it. *Primary*, or baby, teeth that get chipped or knocked out are going to be replaced — courtesy of our good friend Mother Nature. By the time you get your *secondary*, or permanent, teeth, you should be able to take good care of them, since they have to last you about 80 years. Yeah, baby, that's a long time!

GET HELP!

TELL a grown-up NOW to TAKE you to the nearest dentist or emergency room NOW if you or someone else has a permanent tooth that has been loosened, chipped, or knocked out. If the tooth was chipped or knocked out, save the tooth or the chipped piece by picking it up by the non-root end.

To rescue a knocked-out tooth, see OPERATION TOOTH RESCUE, page 123.

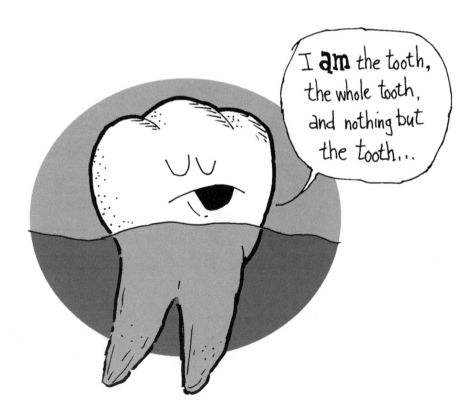

I **am** the tooth, the whole tooth, and nothing but the tooth...

Did I mention ...
PREVENTION?

Keep your teeth (unless soup is your favorite food)

✳ **Wear a mouth guard.** This is an especially good idea if you are involved in a rigorous contact sport or one that involves high speed or hard surfaces. It could save you from accidentally biting your sweet lips, too!

✳ **Follow sporting safety rules.** By reducing the chance of accidents, you might save a tooth or two or three or ... you get my drift!

✳ **Visit your dentist every six months.** The dentist's office is like a health spa for teeth. Healthy teeth are much more likely to hang onto your gums and not get chipped or knocked out. So go!

✳ **Eat right.** A healthy, balanced diet does a body good — and teeth, too. Remember that dairy products like milk, yogurt, and cottage cheese contain lots of calcium that not only make strong bones, but strong teeth, too. Isn't that mooooo-valous? (That was a cow joke!)

Primary (Baby) Teeth

A baby tooth gradually loosens until it falls out. This is a painless event with a very tiny amount of blood that announces that the permanent tooth is moving in. Hurray! For some kids it is such a non-event that they accidentally swallow their oh-so-loose baby teeth with their sandwich! Hey, what was *that?* *Gulp.*

Wiggle Wiggle

The Doesn't-Hurt, Twist-&-Pull, Baby Tooth Removal Trick

If you have a loose baby tooth that is very wiggly and annoying, here's an easy way to remove it!

1. Grasp the loose tooth, using a piece of tissue or gauze for a better grip.

2. Gently give a twist while still pulling gradually. It doesn't take more than a second or two (any longer means the tooth isn't ready yet), and you'll feel a tiny amount of pressure just before the tooth easily pops out. Dab at any small amount of bleeding.

3. If you feel squeamish about removing the tooth on your own, ask a grown-up. Do a little daydreaming while she does the nudging!

4. If the tooth fairy still flies to your neighborhood, don't forget to put the tooth under your pillow.

Permanent Teeth

So, you accidentally took one in the kisser and hurt a tooth. Oh, man, I hate it when that happens!

> ### WHAT TO EXPECT
> **A little pain.** Hey, what'd you expect? That tooth wasn't volunteering. **Some blood.** OK, maybe more than a little. Spit it out so it won't make you queasy.

FIRST-AID TRICKS

Spit to the Rescue!

What if the tooth can't be put back into the owner's mouth? An alternative is to put the tooth in ... are you ready? ... someone else's mouth. Saliva, even someone else's, is the next best substitute to returning a tooth to the home it came from. So in an emergency, have a grown-up tuck the tooth between his cheek and gum, but tell him to be sure not to swallow it!

WHAT TO DO

OPERATION TOOTH RESCUE

Teeth — even those that have been completely knocked out — can be saved, but you've got to act fast. And, it's just as important *not* to do the wrong things, as it is to do the right things. The good news is that you can make a real tooth rescue with a successful ending!

You'll need: The knocked-out tooth, saline solution (contact lens solution or 1 cup/250 ml water plus ¼ teaspoon/1 ml salt), or milk, or saliva, small gauze pad.

1. Take care of the injured person. Look thoroughly for the missing tooth. A tooth that is found — even two hours later — can be successfully implanted by a dentist, **if handled correctly.**

2. Once you locate the tooth (or part of the tooth), **do not pick it up by the root end.** If it is very dirty, rinse it with saline solution (see above), milk, or saliva. **Do not rinse the tooth with drinking water or try to scrub it clean.**

3. Where to store the tooth on the way to the **nearest dentist or emergency room?** In your mouth, right in the socket it came from. (There's no place like home!) Place a small piece of gauze over it and bite down gently to hold the tooth in place. Or, if only a portion of your tooth was knocked out, place it in your cheek between your teeth and your gum. Next best place? Someone else's mouth. A cup of milk will work, too.

I wanna go home!

Nice save! Keep up the good work!

Index

Magnifying glass (small): This is to see your work up close and personal.

Mirror (small): For checking out any eye problems.

Plastic bags (small, resealable): Use these as ice bags in a pinch, or use as plastic gloves if something is kind of icky.

Safety pins: For use with the sling or elastic bandage.

Scissors: For cutting first-aid tape.

Sewing needle: To use with splinters and blisters.

Sling: See pages 113-114 to make your own.

Soap: A small bottle of liquid soap (you can use it even if no water is available).

Soap dish: For storing small items like needle, tweezers, and safety pins. (You could use a plastic bag, too.)

Tissues: Good for bloody noses, tears, and general cleanup.

Tweezers: For all those tweezer-able things like splinters and ticks.

Extras

After Bite Itch Eraser: Buy, or see page 24 to make your own.

Antiseptic wash or a cleanser like witch hazel: Buy, or see page 70 to make your own. Handy if no access to soap and water.

Penlight: To shine a little light on the subject.

Note

We have not included any medicines such as Ipecac (for poisoning), or Benadryl, or even Tylenol. Ask an adult to make sure these are available in *the family's* medicine cabinet, but kids — well, you know the rule: Don't give or take any medications by yourself.

 Mix and match and put together a kit that reflects how you and your family live and play. Being prepared, that's you. Well done!

More Good Books from Williamson!

Williamson's Kids Can!® Books ...

Kids Can!® books for ages 6 to 14 are 128 to 176 pages, fully illustrated, trade paper, 11 x 8½, $12.95US/$19.95 CAN.

....

Parents' Choice Recommended
The Kids' Book of Weather Forecasting
Build a Weather Station, "Read" the Sky & Make Predictions!
with meteorologist Mark Breen & Kathleen Friestad

Parents' Choice Honor Award
The Kids' Natural History Book
Making Dinos, Fossils, Mammoths & More
by Judy Press

American Institute of Physics Science Writing Award
Parents' Choice Honor Award
American Bookseller Pick of the Lists
Gizmos & Gadgets
Creating Science Contraptions that Work (& Knowing Why)
by Jill Frankel Hauser

American Bookseller Pick of the Lists
Oppenheim Toy Portfolio Best Book Award
Benjamin Franklin Best Juvenile Nonfiction
Super Science Concoctions
50 Mysterious Mixtures for Fabulous Fun
by Jill Frankel Hauser

Real-World Math for Hands-On Fun!
by Cindy A. Littlefield

The Kids' Wildlife Book
Exploring Animal Worlds through Indoor/Outdoor Crafts & Experiences
by Warner Shedd

Parents' Choice Gold Award
Dr. Toy Best Vacation Product
The Kids' Nature Book
365 Indoor/Outdoor Activities and Experiences
by Susan Milord

American Bookseller Pick of the Lists
Oppenheim Toy Portfolio Best Book Award
Benjamin Franklin Education Gold Award
The Kids' Science Book
Creative Experiences for Hands-On Fun
by Robert Hirschfeld & Nancy White

American Bookseller Pick of the Lists
Parents' Choice Approved
Oppenheim Toy Portfolio Best Book Award
Summer Fun!
60 Activities for a Kid-Perfect Summer
by Susan Williamson

Selection of Book-of-the-Month; Scholastic Book Clubs
Kids Cook!
Fabulous Food for the Whole Family
by Sarah Williamson & Zachary Williamson

Parents' Choice Gold Award
Benjamin Franklin Best Juvenile Nonfiction Award
Kids Make Music!
Clapping and Tapping from Bach to Rock
by Avery Hart and Paul Mantell

Parents' Choice Gold Award
American Bookseller Pick of the Lists
Oppenheim Toy Portfolio Gold Award
The Kids' Multicultural Art Book
Art & Craft Experiences from Around the World
by Alexandra M. Terzian

The Kids' Guide to Making Scrapbooks & Photo Albums!
How to Collect, Design, Assemble, Decorate
by Laura Check